Contents

Preface

Special days in the church calendar usually delight both pastor and congregation. Churches are filled, choirs sing their best, offerings are large and the whole atmosphere is one of celebration and rejoicing. While few would join the small child who wishes for Christmas or birthday parties every day, special days do warm the heart and stir the religious impulses of everyone.

But there are problems too. What does the pastor say after he has preached Easter sermons five years in succession to the same people? Can the message for a special occasion be made more striking and effective? Can some of the lay people be more directly involved in the proclamation? Is it possible to sustain interest in a special theme beyond one day of celebration?

The plays and sermons in this book are designed

celebrate
with
drama

celebrate with drama

DRAMAS AND MEDITATIONS FOR SIX SPECIAL DAYS

EASTER · ASCENSION DAY
PENTECOST · MISSION SUNDAY
FELLOWSHIP SUNDAY · THANKSGIVING

W. A. POOVEY

AUGSBURG PUBLISHING HOUSE
MINNEAPOLIS, MINNESOTA

CELEBRATE WITH DRAMA

Scripture quotations unless otherwise noted are from the Revised
Standard Version of the Bible, copyright 1946, 1952, and 1971
by the Division of Christian Education of the National Council
of Churches.

Manufactured in the United States of America

to help pastor and people in celebration. Some churches may decide to present each play on the day itself to enrich the worship service. Some may use the drama on the Sunday following to give greater stress to the message of Easter or Pentecost. Some groups may wish to use the plays in organization meetings to prepare for or to reemphasize the Sunday message. Whatever use is chosen, the plays will help Christians to celebrate with drama the great messages of our faith.

The days chosen are those observed in most Christian churches. Easter is *the* holiday for Christians, bringing to a triumphant climax the story of Jesus' suffering and death. Ascension Day has fallen into disuse in some circles, largely because many have not known what to do with such an event. The play, "He's One of Us!" should help clarify the meaning of the ascension for the worshipers.

Pentecost is coming into greater prominence again because of renewed stress on the work of the Holy Spirit. Mission Sunday has no assigned date but most congregations try to emphasize this phase of the church's work. Fellowship Sunday, sometimes called Ecumenical Sunday has replaced Reformation Day in many churches. The play, "This Old House" will fit either emphasis. Thanksgiving Day is a national as well as a church holiday and most Christian groups observe this day in some fashion.

No special plays are included for Lent, Advent, Christmas or Epiphany. The reason is that I have previously written a number of books containing special plays for these seasons. All these books have been published by Augsburg Publishing House and can be obtained from them. (Lenten plays include: *Cross Words, What Did Jesus Do? Mustard Seeds and Wineskins,* and *Six Faces of Lent.* Advent, Christmas and Epiphany plays include: *Let Us Adore Him, Signs of His Coming,* and *Banquets and Beggars.)*

The meditations included with the plays in this book are simply suggestions for the pastor. In most instances the play is sufficient to carry the message to the worshipers but if a special sermon is desired, the printed meditations may suggest a line of approach for the pastor.

Sometimes we take ourselves too seriously in the church. We seek to be solemn and impressive. The title of this book suggests a different attitude—celebrate with drama. The plays are intended to be vehicles through which the joy of the gospel can be brought to the worshipers. They invite us to celebrate with our Lord the good things he has given us.

The Real Resurrection

CHARACTERS FOR 1st SCENE

MR. MILDON: Fairly young father.

MRS. MILDON: Motherly type, but young looking too.

PHIL MILDON: Teen-ager.

MARG MILDON: Teen-ager, a little younger than PHIL.

SETTING

A modern scene, with three or four chairs. Other furniture if desired.

Scene I

(As scene opens, the family walks into the room. They remove their coats, etc.)

MR: Well, here we are, home at last.

PHIL: Yes, church always takes longer on Easter.

MARG: It sure does. All the choirs have to perform and the preacher preaches longer too.

PHIL: Guess he thinks most of the people won't be back for another year and so he'd better give them a long sermon while he has the chance.

MR: It's not just the service that takes so much time. The building was so full today that I thought we'd never get out. And that parking lot was almost impossible. I've had it. *(Flops in chair.)*

MRS: I'll get you some dinner right away, dear. But I didn't mind that it took us a while to get home. It makes you feel so good to see the church crowded. I wish it were like that every Sunday.

MARG: That'll be the day. But the church sure was full. And the flowers were even better than last year.

MR: I suppose we shouldn't complain about a little inconvenience. Besides, Easter is more than crowded churches and flowers.

PHIL: You're thinking of the Easter bunny, aren't you?

MR: No I'm not, and you know it.

PHIL: Sure, we all do. It's the resurrection that makes it important. You know, I wish I'd lived back there, back in the time when Jesus arose.

MARG: Not me. No TV and no cars. And women had a rough time of it then.

PHIL: Oh me, Miss Women's lib, even on Easter. But I didn't mean I would want to be back there all the time. Only, I would like to have seen what happened that first Easter. You know, the look on the faces of those soldiers when they saw that angel. Or the way Jesus' enemies acted when they heard the news of what had happened.

MARG: That *would* have been keen. Wouldn't you like to have been there, Mom?

MRS: Yes, of course. *(Sits.)* I've often thought about those women that went to Jesus' tomb that first Easter. It must have been a shock to them when they found out about the resurrection.

MR: You'd have fallen over in a faint the minute you saw the stone had been rolled away. Wouldn't have done an angel any good to talk to you.

MRS: I guess there's no way I can prove you wrong about that.

PHIL: You know, sometimes I think we get cheated in the church today. *(Sits.)*

MR: Cheated? How? You get your money's worth,

considering how much you put in the collection plate.

PHIL: I don't mean that. But those people got to see Jesus alive after his crucifixion. The women saw him and so did Peter and John and the others. We don't get anything like that. We just get to see each other in the church and sometimes that's not so much.

MARG: But that's what faith is all about, Phil, *believing*, even though you haven't seen.

PHIL: You must have been studying your confirmation lesson. But I still say it would have been better to have been there. If only they had had a movie camera or at least a tape recorder, that would have been something.

MR: I'm afraid there's no use of your wishing, Phil. It all happened a long while ago.

MARG: Well, at least some women got to see Jesus first after the resurrection. Score one for our side. *(Marks it up.)*

MRS: It must have been a wonderful experience for them. The most important thing that ever happened to them or anyone else, as a matter of fact. I'm sure Mary Magdalene and the others remembered every little detail. They probably told people about it every chance they got.

PHIL: Maybe they bored people to death with their stories.

MARG: I doubt that. But they must have been considered important people in the church, then.

MR: They were. People who had seen Jesus alive after the resurrection were witnesses. The church had great respect for them.

PHIL: If I could just have talked to one of them! Even that would be something.

MR: Until they invent some kind of a time travel machine, like the stories in all those trashy magazines you keep reading, you'll just have to be content to be an ordinary Christian, dependent on faith in the gospel, like the rest of us.

PHIL: I suppose you're right.

MRS: I'm afraid he is, dear. But all this talk has started me thinking. It *would* have been wonderful to have lived back in Bible times. I would like to have seen Jesus too, even for a moment, after his resurrection. Well, there's no use wishing. Guess I'd better get our Easter dinner on the table.

MARG: I'll help.

MR: We'll all help. Come on, Phil. Stop dreaming and let's get to work.

PHIL: Okay. But I still think Christians today get cheated. We ought to get a chance to see the Lord too. (*They all exit. The choir sings softly* Jesus Christ Is Risen Today, *or another Easter hymn. During the singing the stage is set for the second scene.*)

Scene II

CHARACTERS

(Four of the characters from the first scene can be doubled in the second but that will demand quick costume changes. If there are enough actors available, it will be better to use different people for the second scene.)

MARY MAGDALENE: A bit dreamy. Middle-aged.

JOANNA: Rather pious sounding. Same age as MARY MAGDALENE.

SALOME: Younger than the other two. A bit more practical.

PETER: Older, rather bombastic but quick in speech.

JOHN: Younger, somewhat dreamy, like MARY MAGDALENE.

HULDA: An older teen-ager, sincere.

SETTING FOR SCENE II

The room is bare. The chairs in the former scene can be covered by pieces of colored cloth or they can be replaced by low benches. There should be places for four or five people to sit. The room is the home of MARY MAGDALENE.

(MAGDALENE is seated as the scene opens. There is a knock at the door. She goes to answer it.)

MAGDALENE: Joanna and Salome! Do come in. So good to see you. *(They enter.)*

JOANNA: The Lord's peace to you and to this house, Mary Magadelene. *(They kiss lightly.)*

MAGDALENE: And to you. You always sound like one of the psalms, Joanna. Salome, it's been a while. *(They kiss, lightly.)*

SALOME: You know I wouldn't miss coming today. But where is Mary? You know, James' mother?

MAGDALENE: She couldn't come. She's not been well and she sent word that we weren't to expect her.

JOANNA: *(Piously.)* She'll be seeing the Lord again before any of the rest of us.

MAGDALENE: You may be right, dear. But let's sit down. Peter and John should be here in a few minutes. *(They all sit.)*

SALOME: I wasn't sure they'd be able to make it. Jerusalem is getting to be a rather dangerous place for all of us.

JOANNA: The Lord warned us that would happen. He said there would be persecution but nobody believed him.

MAGDALENE: *(Drily.)* The Lord told us a lot of things that we didn't listen to very well. But Peter and John won't miss today for anything.

JOANNA: Just think—five years since it all happened.

SALOME: Yes. The time has gone by in a hurry.

MAGDALENE: Not to me, it hasn't. It seems an eternity since we saw Jesus and talked to him. I miss him more every day.

JOANNA: But Magdalene, I talk to him every night in my prayers.

MAGDALENE: Oh, I know. So do I. But it's not the

same. I'm afraid things won't ever be the same for us who knew him until he comes back. *(A knock at the door.)* Oh, there's Peter and John, I suppose. Excuse me. *(Goes to door and opens it.)*

PETER: *(In doorway.)* Magdalene, my dear, let us in quickly. There may be spies in the street.

MAGDALENE: *(Steps aside and* PETER *and* JOHN *enter.)* Come in, then. John, how are you?

JOHN: Scared, I suppose.

PETER: Nonsense. His knees may shake a bit but he'd walk into a den of lions if he thought the Lord wanted him to.

JOHN: No speeches, Peter. *(Seeing the others.)* Joanna, how are you? And Salome?

JOANNA: I'm well, God be praised.

SALOME: So am I.

MAGDALENE: We're all well, except Mary. And we're honored that you're here. Please sit down.

PETER: Thank you. *(He sits.)*

JOHN: I think I'll stand for a while. *(Remains standing as though listening for trouble.)*

SALOME: Joanna was afraid the High Priest and his soldiers might frighten you away.

PETER: Certainly not. Nothing, *(Remembers his weakness for boasting.)* well, almost nothing would make us miss coming here today. We've been to-gether every year since the resurrection.

JOHN: That's right. Five years ago it happened. Five years ago Jesus came back to us from the grave.

MAGDALENE: But only for such a short time.

JOANNA: He'll come again. He promised to return, you know, just as he promised he would rise again. We must have faith.

MAGDALENE: *(Stung.)* I know. You don't have to preach to me, Joanna. And I won't spoil our visit by complaining. It's so good for us to be together again and relive that morning when we learned he had risen.

SALOME: *(Slyly.)* And when certain men refused to believe what some silly women said.

PETER: You'll never forget that, will you, Salome?

JOHN: Perhaps we shouldn't be allowed to forget it.

PETER: I don't think there's any danger of that, at least for me. And I don't need any special re-minder. How blind we all were!

JOANNA: I'll never forget that morning, never.

MAGDALENE: I'm afraid I will.

JOANNA: What!

JOHN: What do you mean, Magdalene?

MAGDALENE: Simply that I'm getting older. All of us

are. And five years is five years. I remember the excitement of that day, of course. I remember that terrible moment of recognition when I heard him say, "Mary" and I realized that the man I thought was the gardener was really Jesus. But I keep trying to remember the sound of his voice and the way the sky looked that morning, and every little detail of what I did and how I felt. And it's all starting to go. I'm beginning to forget.

SALOME: You can't expect anything else, Magdalene. Memories fade.

MAGDALENE: But I don't want this one to fade.

PETER: You make me confess my worries too. It's happening to me, just the way you said. I remember, but not so well.

JOHN: But you can't imprison one day completely, even a day like that. It's been five years. We all get older and we all begin to forget some details.

MAGDALENE: (*Standing and pacing.*) I don't want to forget. I want to keep alive every moment of that day, treasure every word, every gesture. It's the only thing that keeps *me* alive.

JOANNA: Of course you want to remember. We all do. That's why it's good for us to meet like this every year. We can remind each other of what happened.

SALOME: You mean we can live on each other's memories.

PETER: We mustn't forget. The church depends on us to keep telling them what happened when Jesus rose from the dead.

SALOME: And what will the church do, Peter, when all of us are dead? When there are no more witnesses?

PETER: Oh, Jesus will return before that happens.

SALOME: Are you sure?

PETER: Positive. *(Pause.)* No, I'm not. I'm not positive of anything except that I saw him alive after the soldiers crucified him. And that's enough for me.

MAGDALENE: (Sitting again.) We're all so fortunate. Out of all the people who have ever lived, we have seen the Lord. We followed him, even to the grave and we know what happened after that. He came alive again. How did it happen that we were chosen to be witnesses?

JOANNA: God has been good to us. Just as he was to Israel when he chose her from among all the nations of the world.

SALOME: Good to us, yes. But there's always a catch. We have a responsibility to remember and to tell the church what happened.

MAGDALENE: That's why I get so afraid when I start to forget.

JOHN: Someone must write it all down in a book.

PETER: That won't be the same. It'll be hard to tell about all he said and did. Hard to make people realize what he was like. Jesus was a person, not a book.

MAGDALENE: Then we're the only ones who really know the truth. And when we're gone, it'll all be gone.

JOHN: Oh no. I hope not. (*A knock at the door. The group reacts immediately.*)

JOANNA: The soldiers. They've come to arrest us.

PETER: Let me go to the door. If it is someone after us, I'll fight with them and you can all escape out the back.

JOHN: (*Seizing him.*) Peter! You tried violence before and it didn't work. You and I will face them together and put our trust in the Lord.
(*Knocking again.*)

MAGDALENE: Go on. Open the door. (*The women huddle together.*)

PETER: (*Opening the door.*) It's only a young girl. Come in, my dear.

HULDA: (*Entering. The others sit down in relief.*) Thank you. You're Simon Peter, aren't you? I've seen you lots of times when you've been speaking to the believers.

MAGDALENE: Why, it's Hulda. Come, sit down, my dear.

HULDA: I didn't know you had guests. This is such a special day I thought I'd come over and chat a bit.

MAGDALENE: That's nice. You remembered it is the day of our Lord's resurrection. These are my friends who saw the Lord with me. John and Joanna and Salome. I think you know Salome. *(General greetings.)*

HULDA: I'm glad to see all of you. This is a wonderful day for all of us.

JOHN: The best day in the world.

HULDA: It certainly is. Since I've known Jesus, this day has been *so* important to me.

MAGDALENE: But Hulda dear, you didn't know Jesus. You've only been a believer for a few months.

HULDA: What difference does that make? Of course I know him. He's my Lord.

JOANNA: My dear, Magdalene didn't mean you weren't a believer. But we five saw him on the day he was resurrected.

HULDA: I'm sure that was nice. But Jesus is with me every day. I talk to him in my prayers and he goes with me wherever I go. I know he's alive because he lives in my heart. That's more important than having seen him when he was resurrected. Isn't it?

MAGDALENE: Why—why I never thought of that.

SALOME: *Have we been fooling ourselves?* Maybe we're not as important as we thought.

JOHN: Hulda, Jesus must have sent you here today. What fools we've been. What egotistical fools.

PETER: Wait a minute. I've been called lots of things but never an egotistical fool before.

JOHN: Well, you've been called one now. Don't you see, Peter? It's not what happened five years ago that's important. It's now. It's not just that Jesus arose but that he lives. *Every* believer knows the risen Lord. Not just the five of us.

PETER: John, you're right, as usual.

JOHN: No, Hulda, is right.

HULDA: I don't understand. What have I said?

SALOME: You've said the right thing. You see, my dear, we five were worried about what would happen in the church when we were gone. We thought people wouldn't believe unless we were there as witnesses. But it won't make any difference whether we're alive or not. Everyone who has accepted Jesus as Lord knows him now.

PETER: Right. And the real resurrection happens again and again. In people's hearts.

MAGDALENE: Hulda, you're a godsend. Now the *six* of us can talk about our Lord who is risen. For we're *all* witnesses to his resurrection.

(Choir sings Beautiful Savior (Fairest Lord Jesus) *as characters leave the stage.)*

The Death and Life of Mr. X

Romans 6:3-11

There are few things a person can say without fear of contradiction in this life. Invariably when we make a categorical statement, someone will mention an exception to prove us wrong. But we are reasonably safe in saying that man must be born before he can die. Consult the obituary column in a newspaper and it will list Joe Doe, born at x time, died at y time, which will always be later than the day of birth. Look at the tombstones in a cemetery and invariably the birth date precedes the time of death. That is simply one of the facts of existence. You have to be born before you can die.

But the life of a Christian has a strange sequence. For the process here is reversed. A Christian dies before he lives. In fact he *must* die or he cannot live. The biography of a follower of Christ must be entitled: "The Death and Life of Mr. X." As Paul says in our text: "We were buried therefore with him by baptism into death, so that as Christ was raised from the dead by the glory of the Father, we too might walk in newness of life." And these words by Paul are simply an echo of what Jesus implied when he told Nicodemus that he had to be born again, for the old must die before the new can be born.

It is said that in the early church this act of dying was symbolized very dramatically. The individual who was to be received into the church by baptism was completely stripped of his old clothes and entered the baptismal water naked. The old person was dead. Then when the baptism was completed, the new convert was given a new garment to symbolize that now he was a new person in Christ. While this vivid ceremony has fallen into disuse, it is still customary in many mission churches for the new believer to be given a different name than the one he had before. The old person is dead and a new person has come into being.

It isn't too hard to see why we must die before we become Christians. Christianity is a new and radical way of life. It is not a kind of patched up version or improvement of former religions. Thus the old man of sin who is all of us simply is of no use anymore. God didn't send his son into the world to put a little icing on the cake of man's morality. Jesus didn't seek to make a few minor changes in men's conduct in his day. They never would have crucified him for that. Christianity says you can't patch up the old life. It must die. Mr. X must die before he can live.

Did you ever observe a man or woman of about sixty trying to act and look like a teen-ager? Nothing can be more pathetic. No matter how liberally such people use cosmetics, they can't succeed. They need a whole new body and mind for such a transformation. In the same way, the old nature of man simply won't fit the Christian mold. We need a new heart, a new life. The sinful self must die. There is no other way for us to become children of God.

But Easter is not the time to talk about dying. The death of the old man of sin is only incidental, only the first step. It is the life of Mr. X and Mrs. X which is important. Having died to self, the Christian now lives through the power of Christ. This text talks about life and resurrection. The clinching verse is the last one: "So you also must consider yourselves dead to sin and alive to God in Christ Jesus." Paul states this same truth in his second letter to the Corinthians when he writes: "Therefore, if anyone is in Christ, he is a new creation; the old has passed away, behold, the new has come."

And that is the wonderful part of the Easter story. Easter doesn't just say that Jesus Christ was resurrected, it doesn't just say that someday we will be resurrected, it also says that here and now we can have new life through Jesus Christ. Easter is not just the celebration of an event which happened long ago, it is the reassurance of what has happened in our life here and now.

E. Stanley Jones once gave a striking testimony about this new life. On one of his speaking tours a woman asked about the song that he seemed to have in his heart. She wanted the same joy that Jones seemed to radiate. He told her: "It's not my song. It's the song of my guest, Jesus Christ, who lives in my heart." The great evangelist knew the source of his Christian life. It is always the living Lord, who transforms and changes our whole existence.

And this is the real assurance of the truth of Easter. We know that Jesus lives because he lives in us. We know that he is not still buried in some forgotten grave in Palestine because he is alive in our heart. One of the most foolish things Christians try to do at times is to attempt to prove the resurrection. No matter how cleverly we argue, others will find a way to explain away our proofs. It may have been different in the days of the apostles when more than five hundred witnesses could be summoned to declare: "We saw Jesus alive, after he was crucified. We walked with him and talked with him." Yet even with such witnesses, men did not believe. Many refused to accept the truth of a risen Lord.

Our situation then is hopeless if we think we can overwhelm scoffers by our logic. Easter is not something you prove, but someone you experience. A man must die first, must lay aside all his sinful nature and open up his heart to Jesus Christ. Then and only then will he know that Jesus is alive.

Easter is no time for injunctions or appeals. It is a day for rejoicing. It is the day when every Christian can say—I died with my Lord but now by the grace of God he lives with me. The risen Christ is here today in the hearts of all who have experienced his love and grace. Like the early church let us say, "He is risen," and then echo the reply, "He is risen indeed."

He's One of Us!

CHARACTERS

Marta: A secretary, enthusiastic and somewhat emotional.

Darci: A leader in heaven, concerned but not too dignified.

Gaylus: A young man from the earth. Part can be played by a woman.

Sarbin: An older man from the earth, a bit emotional and cynical.

Leah: Sarbin's wife, quiet but positive and strong when she takes charge.

SETTING

An office in heaven. There should be at least three chairs on stage and a small table or desk, covered with file cards. Furnishings should be simple. No effort need be made to suggest that Marta and Darci are angels but their costumes should be a little different than the three from the earth. All characters may wear robes or ordinary clothing.

28

(As the scene opens, MARTA *is sorting cards at her desk. She keeps listening and when* DARCI *enters, she pushes her cards aside, some of which may fall on the floor, and rushes over to* DARCI.)

MARTA: *(Excited.)* Darci, Darci, tell me. Is it true? Is it really true?

DARCI: *(Teasing.)* Of course it's true. Everything is true in heaven. There's no deception here. Even the streets are 24 carat gold, although nobody could tell the difference between that and gold plate. But what are you talking about?

MARTA: Darci, you're such a tease. You know what I'm talking about. The rumor is everywhere.

DARCI: Rumor! Even in heaven we have to have rumors. What is it this time?

MARTA: As if you didn't know. Everyone is saying it. THE SON IS COMING BACK. He is, isn't he?

DARCI: *(Calmly.)* Oh, so that's what you're so excited about. Yes, my dear, the Son is coming back from the earth. That was the main news we received at council meeting today.

MARTA: *(Dancing around.)* O Darci, how wonderful. Everybody has missed him so. It'll be heavenly to have him here again. Just like old times.

DARCI: Not quite. You forget that when the Son went down to earth, he became a human being.

MARTA: Oh, but that was just for a little while, for his visit down there.

DARCI: No, Marta. The Son *became* a human being. He will always be human.

MARTA: *(A bit disappointed.)* Oh well, some human beings are nice, too, although I don't find too many good ones in my card files here. *(Gathers up cards.)* Anyway, he'll always be the Son to us here in heaven.

DARCI: Of course he will. More honored than ever before. The bells will ring when he arrives back.

MARTA: Darci, you must give me time off to see him when he comes. I can't miss it. I can't. I can't. *(Grabs him by the hand.)*

DARCI: You don't have to plead. It's going to be a holiday for everyone. He may even arrive today. But just so you won't be too shocked when you see him, I'll have to tell you that men didn't treat him very well when he was down on the earth.

MARTA: The ungrateful wretches.

DARCI: I'm afraid those are the only words you can use to describe them.

MARTA: They didn't actually hurt him, did they?

DARCI: Prepare yourself for a shock. We learned the whole story at the council meeting today. Men killed him.

MARTA: *(Shocked.)* Oh no!

DARCI: Oh yes. They crucified him and put him in a grave.

MARTA: But Darci, how could the Father allow that to happen. To his only Son?

DARCI: It all has something to do with God's love for man. The Father *did* raise the Son from death, but he still bears the marks of man's cruelty in his hands and his feet. And there's a spear wound in his side.

MARTA: I feel like I'm going to cry.

DARCI: *(Kindly.)* Marta, no tears in heaven.

MARTA: But he'll soon be healed of his wounds, won't he? There's no suffering here.

DARCI: The wounds will remain, forever and ever. They are marks of love now, signs of how precious these human beings are to the Father.

MARTA: Well, it's all very strange.

DARCI: Yes, even in heaven we don't always understand God's ways. We only trust in him. *(Knock on door.)* See who that is. (MARTA *goes to door.* GAYLUS *and* LEAH *are there.)*

MARTA: Yes. What is it that you want?

GAYLUS: Please, is his excellency Darci in? We must talk to him. (MARTA *looks to* DARCI *for instructions.)*

DARCI: Invite them in, Marta.

MARTA: All right. You may come in. Here's Darci. *(Indicating him. The delegation enters and fall on their knees before* DARCI).

SARBIN: Excellency—

DARCI: *(Shocked.)* Here, here. Stand up. You mustn't kneel before me like that.

GAYLUS: But we have a request to make.

DARCI: I'll not hear it until you stand up. *(They all stand. LEAH stands behind the other two.)* That's better. In fact, won't you be seated. Marta, get some chairs.

SARBIN: We prefer to stand, excellency.

DARCI: All right. But I'm going to sit down. And Marta, you take notes. *(She sits close to DARCI with her pad and pencil ready.)* Now my name is Darci. No titles. I know you, Gaylus. But I'm afraid the others are strangers to me.

GAYLUS: This is my friend Sarbin and Leah, who was his wife on earth. We're a delegation from the people who have come here from the earth. And we need your help.

DARCI: I see. Well, this office deals with the problems of people from that planet you call earth. So you've come to the right place. But how may I help you?

SARBIN: Please, first tell us if the rumor is true.

MARTA: *(Breaking in.)* Oh yes, it is. The Son is returning to heaven. He may even be here today.

DARCI: *(Amused.)* Is that the rumor you are inquiring about?

GAYLUS: Yes it is.

MARTA: Isn't it wonderful?

SARBIN: Oh the contrary. It's disastrous.

DARCI: Disastrous?

MARTA: How can you say that?

SARBIN: It's a terrible calamity.

MARTA: I think *you're* terrible. (*Turns back on them. Very angry.*)

GAYLUS: Please, let me explain.

DARCI: I wish you would, before my secretary gets hotter than the regions below.

GAYLUS: It's very simple. You see, we're from the earth, as we said.

MARTA: It's not hard to tell that. Earth people only get into heaven by the skin of their teeth and it always shows.

DARCI: Marta!

GAYLUS: I know that people from earth don't always have a high standing in heaven.

MARTA: You should see my files. Some of your people—

GAYLUS: But that's just the point. You see, we earthlings are weak, sinful, easily led astray. Even the best of us.

MARTA: That's why the Son had to go down to earth. He had to rescue the people from your own trouble and mistakes.

SARBIN: And we are eternally grateful. But if he's coming back so soon, it will all be for nothing.

DARCI: What do you mean?

SARBIN: Simply that men will fall back into their old evil ways again. It isn't enough for the Son to spend a few years on the earth, even though he may have taught men many wonderful truths. He needs to stay on the earth for a long, long while. *(Pleading.)* Don't you see? His work there isn't finished yet.

DARCI: But the Son knows what to do, better than any of us here in heaven do. Better even than you human beings do.

SARBIN: Nobody knows the power of sin like a sinner. If the Son comes back here, who's going to carry on his work?

DARCI: Oh, so that's what's worrying you. You needn't be concerned. Everything has been taken care of. He's appointed some men to spread his message of love and forgiveness to every part of the earth. There are eleven of them, I believe.

SARBIN: A strange number.

DARCI: *(Embarrassed.)* Well, there were twelve but one of the men turned out to be a traitor and sold his Lord to some evil men.

SARBIN: Aha! I have nothing more to say. *(Folds arms and steps back.)*

DARCI: But you mustn't judge the others by that. They're fine men, I'm sure.

GAYLUS: Very wise men? Learned, well trained?

DARCI: *(Obliged to tell the truth.)* Not exactly. They're fishermen and common people. One was a tax collector, so I suppose he had some education. Only, maybe that was instruction in how to cheat people.

SARBIN: *(Who has walked over to the corner, in disgust.)* Aha!

GAYLUS: Do these eleven men have a good leader?

DARCI: Oh yes, a man named Peter. Very loyal. *(Remembering.)* Well, he did deny knowing the Son three times at the time of the trial. And I believe the Lord once called him a devil. But I'm sure he's a good man.

SARBIN: Aha!

GAYLUS: That's not too good a recommendation. But how about the others? Are they brave men? Did they stand by the Son in his trouble?

DARCI: *(Reluctantly.)* Not exactly. The truth is, they all ran and hid when the Son was arrested.

MARTA: *(Shocked.)* Oh, Darci.

SARBIN: Aha!

MARTA: (*Upset.*) Can't you say anything but "aha"?

SARBIN: (*Stepping forward again.*) Yes, I can. And I'm going to say it now. Excellency—Darci—don't you see our problem? We were so hopeful when we learned the Son was going down to earth to rescue our people. It seemed the answer to man's dreams. At last earth was going to get a king who would teach us the truth and who would lead and guide men to better things. We shouted and sang for joy when the news came to us. But this new change destroys all our hopes. We know that we can't expect the Son to stay on earth forever. But if he could only stay for a hundred years, or a thousand years—what are years in eternity— then there would be real hope for men. He could teach men how to behave and could make them obey him. He does have divine power, after all. But he's only been on earth some thirty-three years. That's not enough, not even the beginning of enough. Please, please do something.

DARCI: But what can I do? I'm only one of the councilors. I have no control over the Son.

GAYLUS: But you could go to the council and tell them what we've told you. The situation is hopeless as it stands now. Perhaps the council could even call us in to tell them what it's like to be a human being living in a wicked world. Perhaps the Father would change his plans and have the Son stay on earth for a while. Even if we're too late to prevent his return, the Son might go back to the earth after a short stay here and take charge of things again.

MARTA: *(Boiling again.)* You people from earth take the prize, the solid gold brass ring.

DARCI: *(Slightly amused.)* Oh, oh. You've stirred her up again.

MARTA: *(Taking the center of the stage and lecturing* GAYLUS *and* SARBIN *in turn.)* They certainly have. Isn't it enough that the Son had to go down to your miserable little planet for thirty-three years? Especially when there are thousands and millions of other worlds for him to care for. Isn't it enough that he even became a human being and will have to remain that way forever? Isn't it enough that you earth people mistreated the Son and even put him to death when he was on your earth? And now you want him to stay there for another hundred years—a thousand years, maybe. Is there no limit to your presumption? To your insolence? To your selfishness?

DARCI: *(Impressed.)* You're an eloquent speaker, my dear. Not a polite one, but very eloquent. Maybe you should be on the council in my place.

SARBIN: *(Sadly.)* I'm afraid she's speaking the truth. We are being selfish. We had a dream of a better world, but I guess human beings are hopeless. You are right, my dear.

GAYLUS: We shouldn't have disturbed you. *(They both begin to cry.)*

MARTA: Here, here. Don't do that. I didn't mean to make you feel bad. I only want the Son back in heaven.

DARCI: It seems you've dashed some dreams, Marta. Even provoked tears in heaven.

MARTA: *(Quickly repentent.)* But I didn't mean— Darci, you'll have to go to the council right away and plead for the Son to be allowed to stay on earth.

DARCI: *(Amused.)* You certainly blow hot and cold, Marta.

MARTA: I don't want to be selfish too. If it will help the people on earth—after all, the Son is one of them now.

DARCI: So he is. But gentlemen, are you sure this is necessary?

GAYLUS *and* SARBIN: Oh yes.

SARBIN: We need someone to rule over us. Someone to make us do God's will.

DARCI: *(Turning to* LEAH *who has been standing silently by.)* And you, my dear—Leah, is it? Do you agree with them?

LEAH: No. I don't agree at all.

GAYLUS: What?

SARBIN: I knew we shouldn't have brought her. Don't listen to her, Darci.

DARCI: I'm afraid I must. Here, sit down here. *(Pulls up a chair. LEAH sits down while the men stand and glare.)* Tell me what you think.

LEAH: Thank you. I'm not trying to be obstinate or stubborn. But I believe it would be better for the Son to come back to heaven now.

MARTA: I don't understand. I'm all confused.

GAYLUS: She's simply trying to be different. She wants to start an argument.

SARBIN: Just like a woman.

MARTA: I like that!

DARCI: Will you all be still and let Leah talk? Now why do you think the Son should come back now when Sarbin and Gaylus want him to stay longer?

LEAH: It's very simple. I think they and the rest of the people from earth who sent us to you are insulting God.

SARBIN: How dare you!

LEAH: I know they don't mean to. But after all, God made us human beings, men and women. He made us in his own image. That's what we were told, anyway.

DARCI: That's correct.

MARTA: It's in my records.

LEAH: Then it would seem that God should know best what people created in his image can do.

SARBIN: You're forgetting our sins.

LEAH: No I'm not. But the Son of the Highest went to earth to bring men forgiveness for sins. And I'm sure that he did it. After all, our own prophet told us that would happen. "And with his stripes we are healed." The Son has done what needed to be done. We have forgiveness. And if he will only give men his spirit to guide them—

DARCI: The Father has promised that. His Holy Spirit will be with men on the earth as long as the earth stands.

LEAH: Then I think men, made in God's image, can carry on the Son's work.

GAYLUS: But it would be so much better if the Son were to make sure men make no mistakes.

SARBIN: That's right. Human beings need a master, a king.

LEAH: No. That's where you're wrong. You want God to treat men like slaves who have to take orders or be beaten. But God didn't make us to be slaves. God has always given us a choice, but because of sin, men have been making the wrong choices all their lives. Now things can be different. If men's sins are forgiven and God's spirit is there to help, many human beings will make the right choice.

They will serve God out of love, not from compulsion or fear.

SARBIN: But it will be so hard. The good people on earth are so weak and so few. And there are only eleven men to begin the work.

LEAH: *(Scornful.)* What has man ever gained on earth without a struggle? Man subdued the earth and scratched a living from the barren soil. Man survived the flood and started again. Think of Israel, and how throughout all our history men struggled to keep alive the knowledge of the true God in the midst of idols of the heathen. Now there's going to be a new Israel on earth. And it'll be a struggle again. But with God's help a new and different people will come to be. Men and women will be born again to a new life.

DARCI: It seems she has more courage than you two men.

GAYLUS: And more wisdom, too.

SARBIN: I'm not so sure.

MARTA: *(Sound of bells and shouting.)* Listen. The bells. The noise. He must be back. The Son must be here now.

DARCI: Now for the moment of decision. Shall I ask the council to send him back? Is that what you people from earth want? *(Pause.)*

GAYLUS: No, no. Suddenly I'm not afraid anymore.

He's one of us now. He knows what it means to be a human being. He'll not forget us.

Sarbin: I agree. Let us go and kiss his wounds, suffered for us.

Marta: Darci, I'm shutting up the office for the day. Come, Leah, let's go and greet him. Let's hurry. Hurry. *(Exit.)*

Darci: It's a holiday in heaven. The Son has come back. The whole universe can rejoice now.

Sarbin: Our brother is here. Our brother is here.

(They rush out.)

(Choir may conclude by singing the first verse of the hymn Golden Harps Are Sounding.*)*

God Is Different Now!

Hebrews 4:14-16

One of the most dramatic sections of the Bible is the fortieth chapter of Isaiah. In this very poetic passage God is pictured as looking down on the earth and seeing men as grasshoppers. Indeed everything appears minute to the mighty eye of God, for the nations are "like a drop from a bucket, and are accounted as the dust on the scales." The writer of this passage reflects the common view of God in the Old Testament—he is a God of might and power. Of course there are more tender views of the Creator, even in this same chapter of Isaiah, but generally the God of B.C. is the "wholly other," different from his creation, one who calls for awe and respect.

The New Testament gives us a different picture. God is different there. He is the waiting Father, the Great Lover, the Concerned One who cares for the poor and the weak. The picture is so different from the Old Testament that one of the early heretics insisted that there were two different gods portrayed in the Bible.

We would not agree with that conclusion. But the contrast is great. What makes the difference? Why is there such a sharp distinction between B.C. and A.D.? Of course the answer is one word—Jesus. The picture Jesus gives us of God is much deeper, more personal than anything the Old Testament writers knew. The prophets could talk *about* God; only Jesus could reveal God completely. And perhaps this sharp distinction is best seen in the story of the Ascension.

That may seem like a strange statement. The Ascension of Jesus is often regarded as an embarrassment in the church since it seems to make Jesus, in the minds of some, a kind of early astronaut. Even when we get past that stumbling block the Ascension seems like a triumphant day for Jesus but a rather sad day for us since it took him away from this earth.

And right there we are wrong. The Ascension did not take Jesus away from us, it brought God close. In the Old Testament God seemed different from man, a being beyond man's comprehension, one who could look on man as a grasshopper. But with the Ascension Jesus Christ, born of a woman, is merged into the godhead. He is God and yet he shares our nature. Man was originally made in God's image but in Jesus that image is strangely returned to God himself. God is one of us now.

Did you ever go to a strange community where you didn't know anybody and no one spoke your language? That can be a very chilling experience. But suppose that suddenly you spotted a fellow countryman whom you did know for many years. What a difference that would make. And that is what is symbolized for us in the Ascension. God is now someone whom we know. He is no alien king who sees the inhabitants of the earth as grasshoppers. He is no stranger, he is Jesus, bone of our bone and flesh of our flesh. That's why the writer of Hebrews can speak about our boldness in coming to God. He is someone close to us.

But the Ascension means something more than closeness. It also means understanding. And that's important for without understanding the best intentions can go wrong. Thus workers who go into the slums to help the poor often fail in their efforts because they don't understand. Missionaries were singularly inept in some lands until they studied the native mind and the local customs.

It is easy to feel that God too doesn't understand. If we are only grasshoppers in his sight, little vermin crawling on the face of this small planet, then God cannot appreciate our problems. But as the writer of Hebrews reminds us, Jesus has been here. He has been tempted as we are He has known pain and suffering, loneliness and desertion. He is one "who in every respect has been tempted as we are." So, if man ever had any cause to complain that God does not understand, the Ascension assures us that time is past. The Son of God has been here and knows what human life is like.

Louis Untermeyer once wrote a poem entitled *Caliban in the Coal Mines.* In the poem a miner complains that God can't understand the darkness of the mine for God dwells in a "well-lighted sky." At the end Caliban asks for God to "fling us a handful of stars." But God has done more than that. He has walked on this earth, taking on himself the burdens and problems of humanity. He knows and understands.

But we must see one last picture in the Ascension. This concerns itself with the greatest barrier between God and man—sin. No matter how chummy we may try to get with God, sin always separates us. God is holy and we aren't. Even Jesus, tempted as we are, was "yet without sinning." But the writer of Hebrews gives us another picture—Jesus as the High Priest. And that means he has made the atonement for man's sin, just as every high priest did in the Old Testament. Only of course Jesus himself was that atonement for sin. With his ascension the sin bearer now stands in the very presence of God. He is both judge and advocate for us.

How beautifully our text puts it. "Let us then with confidence draw near to the throne of grace, that we may receive mercy and find grace to help in time of need." We have no cause for fear. Someone has gone ahead to prepare the way. The God who thundered at Mt. Sinai and terrified the children of Israel is still the God of the universe. But we see him differently now. He is the one who loves us and for-gives us. The Ascension of Jesus should not bring us sorrow or indifference but great joy.

A Spy on God

CHARACTERS

HARRY AGRON: Cynical, sneering. The chairman of the group.

MILDRED CUSHING: A bit of a gusher, the kind associated with any movement.

FERN NACHES: Highly educated, cold in her attitude toward others except toward Agron.

BETTY DARVIN: A joiner, not too bright.

JIM HEFNER: An independent thinker, young, likeable.

A READER: Either offstage or at the lectern. Man or woman.

SETTING

The setting is a simple meeting room. All the characters may be seated at a table or a small table may be at one end for the chairman and the secretary.

Scene I

(As the scene opens, the characters are talking to one another. AGRON *calls for order, pounding for attention on the table.)*

AGRON: All right, all right. Let's quiet down. The meeting of the Conron County Atheistic Society will now be in session. Mildred, will you call the roll?

MILDRED: But Mr. Agron, everybody's here. There are only five of us in our society.

AGRON: Nevertheless, call the roll. We should do things decently and properly, even if we are a small group.

MILDRED: Yes sir. *(Stands and calls.)* Harry Agron.

AGRON: Here.

MILDRED: Betty Darvin.

BETTY: Here.

MILDRED: Jim Hefner.

HEFNER: Here.

MILDRED: Fern Naches.

FERN: Present.

JIM: There's always one.

FERN: *(Snapping.)* I see nothing wrong with being grammatically correct.

AGRON: Finish the roll call, Mildred.

MILDRED: Yes sir. Mildred Cushing. *(Looks around*

and then realizes.) Oh, that's me. I'm here. And that's everybody. *(Sits.)*

BETTY: We never seem to have anybody new.

FERN: What do you expect? The people in this county are all idiots. We'll never get any new members from them.

AGRON: Now ladies, let's not get discouraged. I assure you there are more than five atheists in this county, but it's not easy for some of them to stand up and be counted. It's bad for business. And there are lots of church people who say they believe in God but live as though he didn't exist. So we're not alone. Time is on our side.

FERN: Well, I wish time would hurry things along a little. I'd like to see some action here.

AGRON: That's our business, to provide the action. Suppose we begin with our usual report on activities. Mildred, what have you been doing the past two weeks to promote the cause of atheism?

MILDRED: *(Stands.)* Oh, Betty and I have really had a busy time. We've been mailing out copies of our newest pamphlet, "God isn't dead. He never was born." And last Sunday was the most exciting time of all. We went downtown to the biggest church in the city.

JIM: Holy Trinity?

MILDRED: That's the one. On Main and 7th Street, you know. We got there just when the service was ending. It's hard to tell how long church services will last these days. Preachers must be preaching shorter sermons or changing things in the services or something.

AGRON: Get on with your story.

MILDRED: Oh yes. Well, as the people came out we gave everybody a copy of our pamphlet and most everybody took a copy too.

JIM: People will take almost anything if you give it to them free.

MILDRED: Maybe so. But anyway, you should have seen some of the faces people made when they realized it was a pamphlet about atheism.

BETTY: One man threatened to have me arrested and a woman tried to hit me with her pocketbook.

FERN: Fine Christians!

MILDRED: Yes, it just shows. Most of the people threw the pamphlets away and we picked them up because we didn't want to get arrested for littering. But some must have taken our pamphlets home because we didn't collect as many as we gave away.

JIM: *(Disgusted.)* Bully for us.

MILDRED: But now comes the most exciting part.

BETTY: Let me tell this.

MILDRED: All right. I guess you deserve to, since you worked so hard. Go ahead. *(Sits and* BETTY *stands.)*

BETTY: Well, after practically everybody had gone home, the minister came out of the church and locked the door. Then we gave *him* a pamphlet.

AGRON: I'll bet that raised his blood pressure.

BETTY: I'm sure it did. But he tried to be nice. He looked at the pamphlet and started to read it and then when he saw we were watching him, he gave it back to us and said we were misguided women although he knew we meant well and were really searching for the truth.

FERN: *(Scornfully.)* The usual clergy pablum.

MILDRED: He even invited us into his study for a talk but of course we didn't go.

JIM: Why not?

MILDRED: Well, it was getting late and we didn't think it would do any good. And besides we were hungry.

JIM: Lost, one golden opportunity.

AGRON: Now Jim, you mustn't criticize. The ladies did what they thought was right. And who knows? Somebody may read one of those pamphlets and start thinking.

JIM: They'll probably think we're a bunch of kooks. And maybe they're right. *(Disgusted.)* Passing out pamphlets after church services!

AGRON: That will do. We don't dare fight among ourselves when there's so few of us. Mildred and

Betty were doing what they thought was right. Besides, Fern and I must tell you where we've been.

FERN: *(Coldly.)* I'm sure we were doing something more important than handing out pamphlets to a crowd of silly church people.

BETTY: *(Insulted.)* Well!

AGRON: It's not for us to judge. But Fern and I have spent three days at the state capital doing some lobbying.

MILDRED: How exciting.

FERN: It certainly was. *(Stands.)* You see, somebody is trying to get a bill through the legislature to permit prayers in the public schools again.

BETTY: How perfectly awful. Who knows what some of those wild teen-agers will pray for these days!

FERN: *(Scornfully.)* It's not what they'll pray for. It's the whole idea of prayers in the schools. It's an affront to atheists. And we were there to protest. *(Sits.)*

AGRON: We did a good job, too. Talked to a lot of people. It was a little embarrassing when they asked how many members were in our group because those politicians count the votes on every issue. But on the whole, we had a good week.

FERN: I found out politicians are just as stupid as ordinary people.

BETTY: Don't you ever meet anybody who is intelligent?

FERN: Very, very seldom.

BETTY: It must be awful lonely for you.

FERN: Not in the least. *(Beams at Agron.)* Anyway, we did our best.

AGRON: We certainly did. And now we need to hear from Jim Hefner. Tell us what you've been doing the past two weeks to promote our cause.

JIM: I've been thinking. *(Stands and walks as he talks.)*

MILDRED: Thinking?

BETTY: Thinking? What good will that do?

JIM: A great deal of good, I hope. At least thinking makes more sense than handing out pamphlets to people who don't want to read them, or participating in some silly lobby to keep kids from praying. Who cares whether they pray or don't pray?

AGRON: *(Angry.)* Well, sounds like you think you know more than anybody else here. Maybe you'll let us in on some of your *positive* thinking. It's easy to scoff at other people.

FERN: Yes, Mr. Thinker, enlighten us.

JIM: I didn't mean to sound so negative. But I don't think we're getting at the basics here. Our real enemy is the church. As long as people go to church or are in favor of the church we'll never make atheists out of them.

BETTY: That's why we handed out our pamphlets at the church door.

JIM: But that's not the way to handle the problem. Did it ever occur to any of you that churches must have some secret to make it possible to hold people like they do?

AGRON: *(Stands at opposite end of room from* JIM.*)* It's no secret. They just scare people with talk about hell and sin and eternal punishment. They keep their members with the help of a lot of superstitious nonsense.

JIM: I'm not so sure. If it were only superstitious nonsense, people would soon see through it.

AGRON: The church can't last long. It's on its last legs.

JIM: That's what we'd like to think. But men have been saying that for a long time and the church is still there. There must be other reasons why people still go to church.

MILDRED: I think people go to church to have something to do on Sunday.

FERN: That's a silly idea. There are plenty of other things to do on Sunday. People go to church out of habit. A bad habit.

BETTY: I used to go because I liked the music. But

they started bringing guitars into the church and that's when I became an atheist.

JIM: Don't you see? We each have a different explanation but none of us really knows. So when we're attacking the church we're just hitting in the dark. There must be some secret that we haven't discovered yet. And we're going to stay an atheist society with just five members until we learn what's going on and where the church's weak spot is.

AGRON: *(Acidly.)* Just what do you propose to do, Jim? Get the Rev. Mr. Jones down here and torture him until he tells us his secret? Maybe it's something they put in the incense or a special wax they use on the pews.

JIM: You can scoff if you want to. But I propose to do some investigating. I'm going to church next Sunday and keep my eyes and ears open. Then I'll report at our meeting next week and maybe we can get started on some real work that'll make atheism popular in this community.

FERN: Well, it can't do any harm.

AGRON: *(Angry.)* It won't do any good, either. Jim, you'll find the church is full of hypocrites and pious psalm-singing idiots. The service will bore you, the preacher will put you to sleep and then they'll wake you up and try to get you to pay for all the nonsense you've heard. You'll just be wasting your time. Believe me. I know.

JIM: Maybe so. But I'm going to give it a try.

MILDRED: Oh, this sounds so thrilling. I move we adjourn and hear Jim Hefner's report the first thing next week.

AGRON: I suppose there's no use of my opposing *that*. This meeting is adjourned. But you'd better come up with some sensational material next time, Jim Hefner.

JIM: Right. I'm going to be a spy. A spy on God.

(Group leaves the stage and a reader reads the Pentecost story, Acts 2:1-12.)

Scene II

(Same setting as first scene. All the characters are present except JIM. *The center chair is reserved for him.)*

MILDRED: Tonight's the night. I'll bet Jim Hefner will have some sensational news for us.

AGRON: *(Sourly.)* Don't count on it. He thinks he's too smart. Besides, he isn't even here yet.

BETTY: Maybe the church people have kidnapped him and are holding him prisoner.

FERN: Don't be so idiotic. Anyway, here he comes. The big thinker approaches. (JIM *enters.*)

MILDRED: Oh, we're so glad to see you, Jim.

BETTY: We sure are. We were worried.

JIM: No need to worry. I wouldn't miss this meeting for anything.

AGRON: All right, all right. Everybody sit down. Let's get started.

MILDRED: Shall I call the roll?

AGRON: No need to bother with that. You can see everybody's here.

MILDRED: But last time you said—

AGRON: We didn't have anything important to discuss last time. Jim, we're all waiting to hear from you. You promised us some big news and everybody's eager to hear it. Though I'm not expecting much.

JIM: You really do build up my confidence, Harry. Sorry I was late, but I had to do some typing before I came.

BETTY: *(Eagerly.)* Tell us, what did you find out?

MILDRED: Did you learn the secret? Do you know what keeps the church going?

JIM: *(Standing.)* Well, first let me admit that all of you were right in your opinions about the church. Things were as bad as you said they were. The singing was poor and the sermon was dull.

AGRON: Aha. Tell me more. I love to hear people admit that I was right.

JIM: They *were* polite to me. People shook hands

with me when I got there and invited me to come back again when the service was over. A man even helped me to follow the order of worship.

AGRON: Sure. Good public relations to get more suckers in their grasp.

JIM: Maybe. You were right about some of those church people being hypocrites, too. At least I saw people there who've cheated me in business deals and some others who certainly don't sound like Christians when you talk to them on the street.

FERN: You have to be a hypocrite to believe the stuff they hand out in church. Or else a complete idiot.

JIM: I wouldn't exactly say that. But you were probably right about some people coming to church just out of habit. I noticed how some people automatically went to one particular seat but they didn't seem very interested in what was going on. I suppose they've been sitting in the same place every Sunday for years.

AGRON: *(Gloating.)* So you didn't find any great secret after all. The church is just what I said it was —a lot of silly people believing in all kinds of superstitions.

JIM: I didn't say I didn't find any secret. As a matter of fact, I think I did. At least I believe I know now what makes the church strong.

(General murmur—how exciting. Tell us more. This is really an important meeting, etc.)

AGRON: Quiet, quiet, everybody. We're about to hear a great pronouncement. Go ahead, Jim, let us in on the secret.

JIM: All right. But before I do, I want to make sure everything is open and above board and that you really want to hear what I have to say. So I'd like to submit my resignation from membership in the Conron County Atheistic Society. That's what I was typing out before the meeting.

(The news is a bombshell.)

AGRON: *(Standing.)* Your resignation! Jim Hefner, did those people hoodwink you with all their crazy nonsense?

MILDRED: I think I'm going to cry.

BETTY: Me too.

FERN: I feel like I'm going to be sick at my stomach. Put him out of the meeting.

JIM: I'll leave if you want me to. *(Starts to go.)*

BETTY: No, no, let him finish his report. *(Pulls JIM back.)*

AGRON: We'd all die of curiosity if we made him stop now. All right, *Mr. Hefner*, tell us what you have to say.

JIM: It's very simple. I said the singing wasn't good

in church. It wasn't. It would make a real musician tear his hair, or maybe his beard. And the sermon was't a masterpiece. I could probably have given a better speech, or at least made one that was more interesting.

FERN: So! You said all that before.

JIM: I know. But I don't want you to miss the point. In spite of the singing not being so good, there was a power in it that stirred me. And the preacher touched me too. He wasn't trying to sell me anything; he was simply saying what he believed. The strange thing was, the service was ordinary but I was affected by it.

FERN: Just a case of delayed adolescent instability.

JIM: Don't you believe it! I was trying to be as matter of fact as possible and yet I was moved. I couldn't understand what was happening to me. Then I remembered that the minister had read a lesson from the Book of Acts about the first Pentecost in the Christian Church and how the spirit of God had come to them. And the preacher said in his sermon that the same spirit was still at work in the church.

BETTY: Oh, this is thrilling.

FERN: Disgusting woman. This doesn't make any sense to me.

JIM: Don't you see? There's something in the church that's more than the total of all the poor singers and bad sermons and hypocrites and everything else we've made fun of. There's a spirit there, a *holy* spirit who puts meaning into the simple, ordinary things that people do.

AGRON: You must be mad.

JIM: Am I? Let me tell you something else. There were people joining the church that Sunday and when I looked into their faces I saw a peace and contentment that I've never felt, a peace that I've never seen on any of your faces.

FERN: The peace of contented cows!

JIM: Sneer if you want to. But those people in the church have a plus, a something extra that we've never even glimpsed. We've sat here thinking that the church was only an earthly, fallible organization and we've been sure it would crumble as soon as we got our atheistic propaganda working properly. Well, I've learned that's not going to happen. There's a spirit in the church that makes weak people strong and strong people good. They've got a power that unites them and gives them hope and courage whenever they let the spirit speak. I said I would be a spy on God. I was joking then, but I'm not joking now. I've seen God's spirit working among weak, incomplete people. And they've got something I want.

AGRON: So you're joining the enemy?

JIM: I'm not saying that yet. But I've been a fool

long enough, trying to be a great thinker, solving all the problems of life. Now I'm going to find out more about the spirit of God that I saw in the church. And if you have any sense, you'll all come along with me and try to learn too. Good night. *(Exits.)*

MILDRED: Wait for me, Jim. I want to find out about this too. *(Exits.)*

BETTY: *(To* AGRON *and* FERN *who rush toward her.)* Excuse me. Where Mildred goes, I go. *(Exits.)*

AGRON: *(Standing in despair.)* Fools, fools. Can't they see it's all superstitious nonsense?

FERN: *(Bitterly.)* Let them go. They're all idiots anyway.

AGRON: Yes, idiots. But the world seems made up of fools and idiots. We'll never make things safe for atheism as long as these Christians continue with their nonsense. *(Buries head in hands.)*

READER: But others mocking said, "They are filled with new wine."

More Than Meets the Eye

Acts 2:47

In Charles Williams' allegorical play, *Grab and Grace,* one of the characters says, "This boy Grace does most of the work," meaning that our Christian life is centered in God, not in us. MAN, a character in the play, resents the remark and insists: "I will give praise where praise is due, but something is due to me." With those two lines, Williams puts his finger on one of the perplexing problems of Christian faith, the relationship between man's will and God's power.

Luke raises the same question in an even more bewildering way. After picturing the early church at work, preaching, performing miracles, making sacrifices and impressing all by their piety, Luke adds: "And the *Lord* added to their number day by day those who were being saved." One could easily imagine someone in that early church speaking

Williams' lines and saying, "I will give praise where praise is due, but something is due to me."

This is not a stupid theological quarrel that most of us can ignore, either. If God is seen as doing all the work, we are tempted to sit back and say, "Let him get on with it." But the minute we begin to talk about man's efforts in Christian living, we grow proud and start to talk about *our* work, *our* accomplishments, *our* gains. So there is trouble, no matter which way our minds move.

We cannot solve this puzzle in a few minutes, but perhaps there are some things that we can say. Certainly at Pentecost or at any anniversary of the church we become especially aware that there is more than meets the eye in the history of Christianity—there is a power at work behind the scenes. The Spirit of God is always at work in the church. He does not descend on us as a tongue of fire and he may not shake the house with a noise like a mighty wind, but he is at work. The church is always more than the sum of its human membership.

Every honest Christian knows this. In strange and wonderful ways things happen in the church, things that we never anticipated. A word spoken to someone in trouble turns out to be the right word, although we were not aware of any special power or ability. A life is touched by something done, even though we were unaware of being under observation. A prayer is answered in the right way, although it is a way we never thought of. Always, in the work of the church there is more than meets the eye. Someone is behind the scenes.

Dwight Moody, the famous lay evangelist was very aware of the power of the Holy Spirit in his life. When he made his first evangelistic trip to England he experienced great success in winning souls for Christ. A British clergyman told Moody he was delighted with what had happened but couldn't see any connection between what the evangelist had done and the results which had been achieved. Moody was not insulted for he simply recognized another example of the power of the Spirit in the church.

John Bunyan symbolizes this power in *Pilgrim's Progress* by picturing a man pouring water on a fire. But the fire does not go out. Christian, the Pilgrim, wonders at this but is taken behind the scenes where a man is pouring oil on the same fire, thus keeping it alive. That's a picture of the Holy Spirit, the one who gives man's heart help beyond that of human endurance.

And what comfort it should be to us to know that there is a power greater than ours at work in the church. The theater is often called the fabulous invalid, always dying yet never dead, but the church really has a better right to that name. For the weaknesses of believers is so great. Any man can write a book of criticism against the church. Indeed a few years ago this was a popular sport among writers of religious books and the obituary of the church was spelled out again and again. Given our shortcomings, such attacks are understandable.

For the church *is* weak. It is made up of sinful human beings and the best people in the church are none too good. The world usually has the better of it in brains and wealth. Paul remarked that not many wise or powerful had been called into fellowship in his day and that situation hasn't changed much.

What comfort then to know that it doesn't depend on us, to know that there is more than meets the eye in the church, that there is power behind the scenes pouring oil on the fire. What joy to know that the Lord still can and does add daily to the church those who are to be saved. When men assess the church today, they need to remember that they have not completed their task when they have measured the strength and weakness of the members. There is One whose name doesn't appear on any church roles but who makes all the difference in the success or failure of the church.

But the Holy Spirit is always *behind the scenes.* And someone must be on stage. God has chosen to use human beings to accomplish his work. And this is where the picture in the Book of Acts fits in. Those people were not wasting their time, doing the Lord's work, even though he was the one who was adding to the church membership. Neither are we wasting time when we serve God. Somehow, in a way that doesn't meet the eye, God uses sinful men as blunt tools to do his work. Thus Paul could say with a touch of pride that he worked harder than any of the apostles and then add: "though it was not I, but the grace of God which is with me."

And this doesn't mean that we are only puppets, only part of the scenery. For when Christians don't work, nothing happens. When the church grows lazy and corrupt, growth ceases. There is a correlation between our activity and the activity of the One who operates behind the scenes. The hymn "Go labor on, spend and be spent," is just as Christian as the one which proclaims: "Nothing in my hand I bring, simply to thy cross I cling."

And so we haven't solved the puzzle at all, the puzzle of how God is involved in the work of the church. The Christian cannot completely grasp this relationship between the Holy Spirit and believers. All we can do is to remind ourselves that there is more than meets the eye in the church. Our business is to work and testify and serve and let God take care of the rest.

Luke 14:12-14

Missionary in Reverse

CHARACTERS

JASON CARLISLE: A business man, rather narrow in his outlook.

MARTHA CARLISLE: Jason's wife, quiet, a peacemaker.

BETTY CARLISLE: Teen-aged daughter, sharp in criticism.

REV. LORENZO: Dark complexioned, a native of Central America.

SETTING

Rather well-furnished living room. There must be at least four chairs. Tables and other furnishings may be added as space permits.

(As the scene opens, the three Carlisles are all reading. Then JASON *puts down his book, looks at his watch and walks toward the door.)*

JASON: It's time that preacher got here. I can't understand why he didn't want us to meet him at the bus station.

MARTHA: His letter said he wanted to do a little exploring in the city as soon as he arrived, although I really don't know what he meant by that.

JASON: I could take him all over the city in the car if that's what he wants to do. Sounds peculiar to me. Oh well, I suppose most missionaries are a bit odd. Have to be to go off to some god-forsaken place and try to make Christians out of lazy natives.

MARTHA: I don't think you should say that, dear. I'm sure missionaries do a lot of good.

BETTY: *(Eager to get into the argument.)* They do a lot of harm, too. The world would be better off if we all stayed home, minded our own business and stopped meddling with other people's religion.

JASON: What do you mean by that, young lady?

BETTY: I mean missionaries are just part of our way of exploiting people in other countries.

MARTHA: *(Sharply.)* Betty!

BETTY: It's the truth. We've been studying all about it in our history class. Missionaries are a part of our exploitation methods. That's what Mr. Madison said the other day.

JASON: Sounds like a pinko teacher to me. I suppose next you'll tell us the salaries for missionaries are paid by U.S. Steel rather than perspiring church members.

BETTY: *(Disgusted.)* Oh Daddy, I didn't mean that. We have to pay the salaries all right. And the missionaries mean well when they go to a foreign country, but they soften up the natives and make them think all white people are good and friendly. Then along come the exploiters and steal all the nation's raw material and enslave the people.

MARTHA: Betty, I don't think such things really happen.

JASON: She could be right, Martha. But look here, Betty, we agreed to have this missionary stay with us for a few days. So let's not have any of that exploiter stuff while he's here. By the way, how long is he going to stay?

MARTHA: The letter said "just a few days until we can make other arrangements."

JASON: Other arrangements? That sounds odd too. Anyway, Betty, keep your speeches for your class in school.

BETTY: *(Angry.)* Oh all right. It's easier to bury your head in the sand, I suppose. But I'm staying out of his way while he's here.

MARTHA: You must be polite to him, Betty. I'm sure he's a fine, sincere man.

BETTY: Oh, mother, you always believe the best about everybody.

JASON: Maybe it would be better if the rest of us did that too. But it's pretty hard in this cutthroat world. By the way, what's this man going to do while he's here? Speak at the church or something? I hope we're not in for a long talk and thousands of slides of half naked natives.

MARTHA: I'm not sure myself what he's going to do. Rev. Nelson was kind of mysterious about the whole business and that letter we received from Rev. Lorenzo didn't help either.

BETTY: *(Jokingly.)* Maybe he's a spy. Maybe he's gone over to the opposition and is coming here to convert us all to be heathen.

MARTHA: Oh Betty! Such an imagination. *(Sound off stage.* MARTHA *gets up.)* I thought I heard a noise outside. *(Knock on door.)* That must be him. Open the door, dear.

JASON: All right. Now Betty, no cracks.

BETTY: I'll be as silent as my hi-fi—*(They look at her.)* when the power's turned off.

JASON: *(Opens door.)* Rev. Lorenzo?

LORENZO: This is the Carlisle residence? *(No effort should be made by Lorenzo to speak with an accent.)*

MARTHA: *(Goes to door.)* Come right in, Rev. Lorenzo. *(He enters.)* I'm Martha Carlisle. We have been expecting you.

LORENZO: You are very kind. *(Sets his suitcase down and shakes hands with her.)*

JASON: Welcome. I'm Jason Carlisle and this is my daughter Betty.

BETTY: Hi.

LORENZO: *(Shakes hands with* JASON *but* BETTY *ignores his outstretched hand.)* I'm pleased to meet all of you.

MARTHA: Please sit down for a few minutes before we show you to your room.

JASON: Yes, you must be tired. I could have met you at the bus station and saved you all the trouble of coming out here by yourself. *(They all sit, with* LORENZO *in the center and* BETTY *off to herself a bit.)*

LORENZO: It would have been nice of you to stop for me. But I wanted to get a quick glimpse of your city before coming here. I looked around quite a bit, particularly at the section south of the bus station.

JASON: That's not a very pretty part of town I'm afraid. Lots of Mexicans and Puerto Ricans there. We have better looking sections of the city, I assure you.

LORENZO: I'm sure you have.

MARTHA: Can I get you a cup of coffee or something to eat, Rev. Lorenzo?

LORENZO: Not just now, thank you. I stopped at a small cafe in the area where I was exploring. I wanted to see where the people ate and talk to some of them.

JASON: You probably found the cafe terribly dirty.

LORENZO: No, not really. The people seemed to be doing the best they could with what they had.

JASON: Some of them don't seem to have much, or to want much either.

LORENZO: That may not be entirely their fault.

MARTHA: (*Steering away from subject.*) Tell me, Rev. Lorenzo, where is your home.

LORENZO: I come from a small city, El Cito, in the part of the world that you Americans call Central America.

JASON: No, no. She doesn't mean where is your mission station. Martha wants to know where you were born. Where did you live before you became a missionary?

LORENZO: I'm afraid my answer is the same. This is the first time I have ever been away from El Cito.

BETTY: But aren't you a returned missionary, come back for a breather in the United States?

LORENZO: Did Rev. Nelson tell you that?

MARTHA: No, but we just assumed that. He said a missionary, come to stay with us.

LORENZO: Ah, Rev. Nelson has kept my secret well. He said he would keep everything *(Pause.)* as you say, under his hat until I got here. My friends, prepare yourselves for a strange and wonderful story of how God works.

BETTY: Say, what is this?

LORENZO: You'll understand in a few minutes. You see, about six months ago a man from Mexico visited relatives in this city and when he went back home he wrote a letter to the local newspaper. The letter told how there were many Spanish speaking people who had settled in this community and how they were having a struggle. They had no church of their own and no one to look after their interests. It was a very sad letter. Well, the newspaper containing this story was mailed to one of our church members in El Cito and he read the letter in church one Sunday. It made everyone unhappy to hear such a report but the hand of God was in all of this.

JASON: I don't see where all this is getting us.

MARTHA: Do be quiet, Jason, and let Rev. Lorenzo tell his story.

LORENZO: Thank you. The members of the church were very shocked and sorry to hear that there were people in your very city who had no one to tell them about their Lord and Savior. And then someone said—let us send them a missionary. We must take the gospel to these people. It was like a story from the Book of Acts. For you see, we had once profited by having missionaries sent to us. Now we were going to be the senders.

JASON: Somehow I don't like the sound of this.

LORENZO: *(Enthusiastically.)* You will, you will. You see, the congregation voted to send me, their pastor to preach the gospel here in your city. It was the only choice since I was almost the only one who could speak English as well as Spanish. And they took up a sum of money to pay my way. So here I am, as a missionary in reverse, as you might say. Isn't it wonderful what God has done?

MARTHA: It sounds very strange to me.

BETTY: I never heard anything like this before.

JASON: *(Standing up.)* I think it's ridiculous.

LORENZO: *(Also standing.)* Ridiculous? Oh no. How could it be ridiculous?

JASON: I'll tell you how. We're a Christian country, here in the United States. We have churches that can take care of the people living here. We don't need any missionaries.

LORENZO: Pardon, but are the people I saw today being served by the church?

JASON: Well, no, not exactly. We did make an effort to get some of them to come to church—the better ones in the community. But they really weren't interested.

MARTHA: It was so hard for them to understand our ways. They didn't have nice clothes to wear to church and many of them didn't know any English at all.

BETTY: *(Getting into the center of things.)* Let me tell you the truth, Rev. Lorenzo. The churches here didn't want the Latin people in their services. The people who live on the south side are poor and can't contribute anything to the church. Riffraff some of the church people called them.

LORENZO: Is this so?

MARTHA: Partly, I'm afraid.

JASON: Sure it's so. And they are riffraff, lots of them. My factory is located in that part of town and I know what the people are like.

LORENZO: I'm glad to hear what you tell me. These people then need the gospel and since no one else is serving them, I won't be stealing sheep from others. It is right that I should be here.

JASON: No, it's not right. Look, Dr. Lorenzo, we Americans send missionaries all over the world. We pay thousands of dollars for their salaries. We probably pay too much for our mission work. But it's an insult when your people send a missionary to us.

LORENZO: We didn't think we were being insulted when you sent people to preach the gospel to us.

JASON: That's different.

BETTY: Boy, that's a real snappy answer, Daddy.

JASON: *(Angry.)* You keep out of this, Betty. I suppose, Rev. Lorenzo, you'll be expecting us to support you while you work in our slums.

LORENZO: Oh no. The people from my church have paid my way here. They made great sacrifices so I could come. They promised me some more support but I hope to get a job and take care of my own needs while I work for the Lord here.

MARTHA: Surely we can help some. Our church can help.

JASON: Not if I have anything to say about it.

LORENZO: Why are you so opposed to all this, Mr. Carlisle? It seems to me that God has guided me to this very spot.

JASON: If he has, he's made a mistake. Mission work is something done in heathen lands. Greenland's icy mountains and all that stuff.

LORENZO: No no. Mission work, Mr. Carlisle is one person helping another, particularly helping him to know Jesus Christ. And that's all I hope to be doing—helping people to know more about Jesus Christ.

BETTY: Maybe you'd better start in our church, Rev. Lorenzo, rather than down among the Latin people.

JASON: That'll be enough of that.

MARTHA: *(The peacemaker, seeking to avoid trouble.)* Rev. Lorenzo, perhaps it would be better for you to go up to your room now. You must be very tired. Then we can discuss your work a little more when you are rested.

LORENZO: You are very kind, Mrs. Carlisle. But I have been thinking—maybe it would be better if I found a place right away in that section that I explored today. I passed a small hotel and if I took a room there I wouldn't be imposing on your hospitality. I think Mr. Carlisle would feel better if I didn't stay here.

MARTHA: Oh dear, I don't want you to do that. He is welcome to stay, isn't he, Jason?

JASON: *(Sulkily.)* Yes, he's welcome to stay. But I'm not agreeing with his silly idea of starting a mission there on the south side.

LORENZO: *(Firmly.)* I believe it will be better for everyone if I take my leave now. Perhaps later you will see my work differently.

MARTHA: *(Reluctantly.)* Well—perhaps it is for the best, if you want it that way.

BETTY: *(Coming center stage.)* Rev. Lorenzo, before you go, tell me, are you going to need some help in that new mission you're hoping to start?

LORENZO: Miss Betty, everyone needs help. I'm sure I'll need all the help I can get. I'm not at all familiar with your American ways or customs.

BETTY: Well, I've only had two years of high school Spanish and I'm a bit rusty even on that, but I can run errands and baby sit and help people in lots of ways, I think.

LORENZO: If your parents will let you help, I will be very grateful.

JASON: *(Sarcastically.)* Aren't you afraid you're going to be part of the exploiters of the world? Aren't you afraid you'll be doing more harm than good?

LORENZO: I don't understand.

JASON: Then I'll explain it. Just before you came, Rev. Lorenzo, this young lady was telling us that missionaries were exploiters. They were a menace to society and should keep their gospel at home.

LORENZO: *(Bewildered.)* Is this so?

BETTY: Yes, yes I said it. But I'm not too stubborn to admit I was wrong. The church has always seemed hard and self-concerned to me, even when it sends out missionaries. It seems like it's busy counting noses and souls won. But when you said mission work is one person helping another, particularly helping him to know Jesus Christ, then you show me how wrong I've been. If that's what mission work is, I want to be a part of it.

LORENZO: My dear, I will welcome your help. As soon as I get settled, I'll get in touch with you.

BETTY: I'll bring some of my friends, too. I know some of them will be willing to help.

LORENZO: Very good. Then I will be on my way. It's been a pleasure to meet all of you. *(Picks up his suitcase.)*

MARTHA: I do wish you would stay.

JASON: Rev. Lorenzo—

LORENZO: Yes?

JASON: Just now my daughter admitted she'd been wrong, something she doesn't do very often. Would you take an apology from me, too?

LORENZO: No apology is needed.

JASON: Oh yes there is. I said some nasty things and I'm sorry. I guess your coming hurt my pride a little. I've always thought of mission work as something someone does far away. Never could see much sense in it but I gave money for missions when the church pestered me enough about it. But when I see my daughter getting enthused about doing God's work, here in town, it strikes home. You said mission is people helping people. Well, I go for that. And people are everywhere.

So I guess you have to work with them everywhere, with the best tools that you have.

LORENZO: You say it very eloquently, Mr. Carlisle.

JASON: I want to do more than talk. Stay with us Rev. Lorenzo and let's plan together. I can help you in this community. I know I can—if you'll have my help.

LORENZO: It is the Lord who calls helpers into his Kingdom, Mr. Carlisle. And I know he will welcome you.

MARTHA: And I'll help too.

JASON: Then Martha, Betty, we're going to be missionaries too.

MARTHA: Thank God for that, and for you, Rev. Lorenzo.

LORENZO: *(Pleased.)* You see, a missionary in reverse isn't such a bad thing after all.

Why Are We Here?

Luke 14:12-14

There is an old and cruel joke about a minister who preached to the inmates at a mental institution. The minister began with the question: "Why are we all here?"

Whereupon a man who seemingly had more sense than the speaker replied: "Because we are not all there." A rather fitting reply which included the speaker too.

But if we overlook the inappropriateness of the question for the occasion, we will realize that the minister's question is an important one. Why *are* we here? In this life? On this earth? At this particular time? The problem of finding meaning for our existence is a terribly important one for many people.

Young people certainly ask it. What's life all about? I need to find myself. What am I to do with my life? Hearing no answer to such questions, many young people lapse into drugs or mind-blowing music or even end up as suicides. And teens don't have a monopoly on this kind of thinking. Older people, looking back on their lives often feel the same kind of frustration. What's it all about, they ask. We all understand what prompted someone to say, "Life is so daily." The battle against inflation, traffic woes and job monotony often ends with alcohol and sleeping pills.

Well, what *is* it all about? Why are we here? What's the meaning of our existence? Jesus gives us a very simple answer. You may not like it. You may want to argue with it or reject it, but Jesus says we are here to help others. We live so that others may live. Our guiding watchword is service or mission. And life has no real meaning until we recognize this truth.

The setting in the text offered Jesus a good chance to make such a statement. He was attending a dinner party, the kind that people give for their friends, the kind that makes the friends say, "The next dinner is on me. I owe you one." Jesus didn't condemn such a gathering but he pointed out that there was no "giving" involved. It was simply a trading of one menu for another. And then he indicated that if people really wanted to do something of value, they should give a dinner for those who couldn't repay. Be of service to others. Help those who need help. That's the way you find real meaning for existence.

This isn't the only instance where Jesus gives such advice, either. When his disciples get to arguing over who gets first place in the kingdom, he tells them that the one who would be great must be the servant of all. Jesus washes his disciples' feet at the Last Supper and then tells them they must be willing to render such service to one another. In the description of the great judgment scene at the end of time, he pictures the judge as speaking about service—clothing the naked, feeding the hungry. And perhaps the climax comes when our Lord declares on several occasions that the man who would save his life will lose it, only the one willing to lose his life will save it.

So Jesus' witness is clear. You and I are here to help others. Our purpose in life is not to make money or have a good time or earn fame in society; our purpose is to serve others, to be of assistance to those who need help. The old story, "He ain't heavy, he's my brother," is a good description of life for all of us since all men are our brothers and we are here to help them.

Having said that, let's be honest and admit that we don't like the picture too much. We are, by virtue of our sinful nature, self-centered and we tend to focus on our own needs and desires first. What's in it for me? What do I get out of it, we ask. We are all familiar with the little poem in which the man prays for his family and ends by asking for blessings for "us four, no more." Even when we have been saved and redeemed by Christ the old Adam still remains, prompting us to think of self before we think of service.

Yet when we evaluate life carefully, we learn that

those who serve are the ones who are blessed. Happiness doesn't come from selfishness but from self-sacrifice. The Lord still loves the cheerful giver and that doesn't mean money but life. Charles Dickens portrays this so well in his story, *A Christmas Carol* when he shows Scrooge as a man completely self-centered and miserable. Only when Scrooge learns to be of service to others does he become the bubbling, jovial figure that he is at the end. In real life the picture is the same. Who is the happier figure, John Paul Getty in his lonely home in England, with all his billions or Albert Schweitzer, caring for the sick in Africa? Who was the happier, the Apostle Paul who reached the point where he no longer lived but Christ lived in him or the rich young ruler who went away sorrowfully from Christ's presence? Man finds no real joy until his life is lived God's way.

Probably this is the truth which is so often neglected when we talk about missions in the church. We speak about how others need the gospel or we describe the suffering and misery in foreign lands and how we must help these people. All that is true. But the real point of mission is that God placed us here to help others. Mission is not a point for discussion. We are not called on to decide whether we shall do it or not. If we are children of God, we help others. That's what we're here for. That's what the church is here for. Our problem is to get busy and do it.

But there is a very strange ending to this text. Jesus says that while those whom we help will not be able to pay us back, God will do so. And such an idea seems very disturbing to most of us. We have been told that we are saved by grace. We have been informed that we can do nothing to affect our salvation—God has done it all through Jesus Christ. And now comes this promise of reward. Is Jesus contradicting all of our carefully developed theology? Is he espousing a kind of do-it-yourself religion?

Hardly. But our Lord does know what happens when we help others in this life. All too often we are rewarded with—ingratitude. After all, only one of the ten lepers healed returned to thank Jesus. And we may be lucky if we run that high a percentage. The world's attitude is usually expressed by the man who was reminded of how much his friend had done for him over the years, including saving his life, but who replied: "What have you done for me lately?" Mission does not always bring a response of gratitude.

But our Lord reminds us that God does not forget. He is not ungrateful when we are faithful to our purpose in life. This has nothing to do with our salvation. That we do receive through God's grace. But when we serve our fellow men, we can grow discouraged at their reaction. So we are reminded here that God does not forget. And in the words of one of our hymns: "The Master praises—what are men?"

A plow is made to turn up the earth for farming. A stamp is printed to be used to prepay postage on a letter. A lightbulb is manufactured to illumine an area of this world. You and I were created for mission, to help others in this world. And we will find happiness only when we do what God intended us to do in this life.

This Old House

CHARACTERS

THE READER: Can be either a man or a woman.

MARIA: Old, but still with plenty of fire.

NORMAN: Young, idealistic, inclined to argue.

COLETTE: Young, a bit more fanatical than NORMAN.

ANGUS: Large, powerful, bent on destruction.

PATRICK: Same disposition as ANGUS.

RUTH: Solid, conservatively dressed.

SCENE

An interior room in the house. There should be a table where blueprints can be spread out. There should be some pictures and other decorations on the walls or on small tables. Other furnishings can be added as desired. The brief scene at the end can be presented at the front of the stage without changing the scenery.

(As the scene opens, the stage is set but there are no characters present. THE READER steps to the lectern or reading stand and begins.)

READER: This is the story of a beautiful house and what happened to it. The house was built many centuries ago and over its doorway was a sign inviting all the people of the world to come and live there. The greatest architect of all times designed the building, although there were some who said he was only a common carpenter. His house stood at the crossroads of life for many centuries, but as the years passed, some of the inhabitants grew discontented with the way the house was run. And so, one day—

(READER disappears and NORMAN rushes onto the stage.)

NORMAN: *(Calling loudly.)* Maria, Maria. Where are you, Maria?

MARIA: *(Appearing.)* I'm here. What's all the noise about?

NORMAN: I want to talk to you. I've got a complaint to make.

MARIA: I might have known. All you young fellows are full of complaints. What do you want, Norman? More money? Better rooms?

NORMAN: Nothing like that. Maria, can you guess where I've been?

MARIA: Now look, Norman, I don't have time to play

guessing games with you. I've got work to do, even if you haven't. *(Starts to leave.)*

NORMAN: *(Restrains her.)* Wait a minute. I'll tell you. I've been up in the attic.

MARIA: *(Shocked.)* Norman, you know you're not supposed to go there without my permission.

NORMAN: Well, I went anyway, and look what I found. *(Holds out roll of blueprints which he had been concealing.)* The blueprints of the great architect. The plans that he made for this house.

MARIA: *(Scared.)* Give them to me immediately. You have no right to have those blueprints, no right even to look at them.

NORMAN: And you had no right to hide them in the attic. The blueprints should be on display all the time so everyone can see them.

MARIA: *(Recovering herself.)* We can discuss that later. Right now I demand that you give me those blueprints.

NORMAN: Well, you're not going to get them. Not until we've had a little talk, anyway.

MARIA: *(Loud tone.)* Norman!

NORMAN: You can shout if you want to but that doesn't scare me because I've found out some *very* interesting things just by looking at these blueprints. Maria, you've made changes in this house. You haven't kept things the way the great architect intended them to be. *(Threateningly.)* Have you? Have you?

MARIA: Now Norman, you mustn't accuse me like that. Nothing's been changed—and besides I have the right to make any changes that I want to.

NORMAN: Maria, don't lie to me.

MARIA: All right. I'll admit that there've been some minor additions. I've put up some pictures and decorations that weren't mentioned in the original plans.

NORMAN: And what else?

MARIA: Well—I'll admit we do have a bit more ceremony at meals and when we go in and out of the house. But those things don't do any harm and the people who live in the house like them. You're not objecting to a few pictures or ceremonies, are you?

NORMAN: No, pictures or decorations or ceremonies don't bother me. I can take them or leave them alone. But there are some changes that *are* important. Things have been added to our house, Maria, bad things that don't belong here at all.

MARIA: That's not so. I deny it.—What are you talking about?

NORMAN: I'll show you. Come take a look at this blueprint. *(Spreads it out on the table.)*

MARIA: *(Starts to leave again.)* I don't have time for this foolishness.

NORMAN: *(Pulls her to table.)* Now look. Look carefully. *(Points.)* This is the big assembly room for everybody. That's the way it's marked here. Do you see any difference between this drawing and the way the room is now?

MARIA: *(Turns her head away.)* No. None at all. The room is in the same place as it always was.

NORMAN: Of course it's in the same place. You're just being stubborn. *(Makes her look.)* See. There are doors all around the room in this blueprint. Everyone can get into the assembly room from any part of the house. But that's not the way it is now. You've put a wall up here so that most of the people can't get in. Only those who live in the special apartments have access to the assembly room now. Can you deny that?

MARIA: No. I suppose there is a difference. But Norman, *you* can go into the room any time you want to.

NORMAN: That's not the point. You've put up a barrier where there wasn't supposed to be any. And it's got to come down.

MARIA: Now Norman, be reasonable. There weren't many people living in the house when it was first built. Maybe it was all right for everyone to go into the assembly room then. But you can't have everybody traipsing in and out now. The furnishings will get dirty and worn.

NORMAN: The room was supposed to be for all the people. Every one of them.

MARIA: But you and I represent the people. Isn't that enough?

NORMAN: No. The wall has to come down, and I'm going to see that it is destroyed. But first, let me show you something else. *(Points out on blueprints.)* Look over here at the recreation room.

MARIA: You're not going to tell me things have been changed there. Everything is just the way the architect designed it.

NORMAN: Yes, with one exception.

MARIA: What's that?

NORMAN: You're charging admission to the room. That's what.

MARIA: Well, of course I am. We have to have some money to keep things going.

NORMAN: To keep you well fed, you mean. Maria, the architect gave his life for this building. He intended it to be a place of blessing for everyone, but he particularly loved the poor people, the beggars, the widows and orphans. And he endowed the whole house so everything would be free. There aren't supposed to be charges for anything.

MARIA: Oh, you're so idealistic. All you young radicals are.

NORMAN: Is it idealistic to want to keep things the way they were intended to be?

MARIA: Yes it is. Besides, the architect left me in charge. It's my business to make changes when I think they're necessary. I have the authority to do that.

NORMAN: You have the authority to keep the building the way the architect designed it. That's all. Nothing is to be changed until the architect returns someday.

MARIA: *(Disgusted.)* Oh you make me tired. I can't waste any more time with you. After all, you're just one person complaining, and if you don't like it here, you can go live someplace else.

NORMAN: *(Defiant.)* Is that so? Let me tell you, I've got some friends in the house and they've seen the blueprints too. They feel just the way I do. I'm going to call them and we'll see whether you can put me out or not. We're going to take down that wall and get rid of the other changes you've made in the house. And you won't stop us. *(Calls.)* Colette, Angus. Come here and tell Maria what you think.

COLETTE: *(Appears immediately.)* I've been listening to all you've said and Maria, Norman is right. Things in this house have got to be put back the way they were. *(To* NORMAN.) Have you started taking down the pictures?

NORMAN: Oh Colette, the pictures aren't important.

COLETTE: Yes they are. They must come down because they aren't mentioned in the blueprints.

NORMAN: *(Exasperated.)* Taking down pictures isn't the real change that's needed.

ANGUS: *(Appearing with an axe or crowbar.)* Here I am, Norman. I stopped to get my tools. Where should I start tearing down the building? Or do you think it would be easier to burn the whole structure and get rid of it that way.

NORMAN: Angus, we're not going to tear the whole house down.

ANGUS: Oh yes we are. There's no point in trying to repair this old house, especially now that we've got the architect's plans. It's easier to get rid of everything and start all over again.

NORMAN: There's no need for such violence. You'll only make a lot of people unhappy who love this old house. Maria, I didn't say anything about destroying the building, did I?

MARIA: Don't talk to me. I'm just listening to you three quarrel.

COLETTE: We mustn't quarrel or we'll never get things set right again. Angus, Norman's right. The house stays. But the pictures and all the fancy ornaments have to go.

NORMAN: *(Frantic.)* You're both missing the whole point of what I've been saying.

ANGUS: I don't intend to stand around and argue. I'm going to tear this place down. Stand back, everyone.

MARIA: *(Taking charge.)* No you don't. I've got some friends in this house too. *(Calling.)* Ruth, Patrick, I need your help.

PATRICK: *(Appearing.)* I've been listening and just waiting for you to call. They'll not start trouble while I'm here.

RUTH: *(Enters.)* I'm on your side, Patrick. What do you want us to do, Maria?

MARIA: These three want to destroy our beautiful house. See, Angus has an axe and the other two are going to help him. Are you going to let them do it?

RUTH: Certainly not.

PATRICK: It'll be over my dead body. *(Glaring.)*

ANGUS: Maybe I can accommodate you. *(Glaring back.)*

NORMAN: Now wait a minute. Patrick. Ruth. No one wants to destroy this house. *(Looks at ANGUS.)* Well, practically no one. We simply want to put things back the way they were when the architect first built the house.

RUTH: I like things the way they are now.

COLETTE: The house is all right. But the pictures and ornaments have to go. They weren't part of the original plan.

PATRICK: So? We've improved on the plan.

COLETTE: You have no right to change things.

MARIA: Yes we do.

NORMAN: No you don't. But it isn't the pictures that cause the trouble.

ANGUS: I'm not going to stand here arguing anymore. I'm going someplace and start chopping. *(Exit.)*

PATRICK: He's not going to chop into anything. I'll put a stop to that nonsense.

MARIA: Good. Follow him. But watch out. He's a fanatic and such people are dangerous.

COLETTE: While he's chopping away, I'm going to take care of some of those silly ornaments. *(Exit.)*

RUTH: She's going to ruin our beautiful house. Why can't people leave things alone? But I'll put a stop to her.

MARIA: You have my blessing. Go after her, girl.

RUTH: Don't worry, Maria. I'll fix her and some of the others in the house will help me. *(Exit.)*

MARIA: Well, Norman, you see what you've started by your poking around in attics and by your stubbornness.

NORMAN: My stubbornness! If you had let things stay the way they were intended to be, there never would have been any trouble. You're the one who's stubborn.

MARIA: I might have known you'd say that. Well, let me tell you, this house is going to stay the way it is. I might have listened to you at first but now my mind's made up. You're not going to make any changes here. Not even one small one.

NORMAN: We'll see about that. I'm going to get rid of that wall that keeps people out of the assembly hall, even if I have to tear it down with my bare hands.

MARIA: You're not going to touch that wall. I'll put you out of the house if you start anything.

NORMAN: You can't put me out. The architect said anyone could live here who wanted to and I'm going to stay.

MARIA: You wait and see. (NORMAN *exits.*) I thought he was such a nice boy. Now look what he's started. I'd better get busy before those young radicals stir up more difficulty. (*Exit.*)

READER: And that's how trouble began at the beautiful old house. First harsh words and then harsh deeds. And soon, at the crossroads of the world there stood not just one house but many, each looking strangely like the others and each insisting that it was the original house as designed by the great architect. You can read all about what happened in the pages of history. Many people were confused by all of these houses, not only because they looked alike but also because the people who lived in them didn't reflect the spirit of the great architect who loved all men, especially the poor, and who wanted men to love one another and to be one brotherhood. What happened was very sad, and no doubt the architect grieved when he looked down at the house or the houses he designed. But lately, things are different. Something good seems to be happening to the people who live in the houses.

(The characters walk along at the front of the stage. When they finish their dialogue they step back and let the others take their places.)

NORMAN: Hello, Maria. How good to see you. *(They shake hands.)*

MARIA: Norman, you're looking well. That makes me happy.

NORMAN: It made me very happy to be able to visit you last Sunday.

MARIA: It was good to be together again, even for a little while, after all these years.

NORMAN: You are coming to visit me next Sunday, aren't you?

MARIA: I wouldn't miss it. You know, I've been noticing lately how much our houses look alike. I guess I concentrated on the little differences too much and forgot how close we really are.

NORMAN: You're not the only one that made that mistake. But look, here come Colette and Patrick strolling together. (COLETTE *and* PATRICK *enter, arm in arm.*)

MARIA: My, my. I never would have believed it possible. Let's listen to them. *(They step aside and give the others the center of the stage.)*

COLETTE: You know, Patrick, if we work together, we certainly can do a lot more good.

PATRICK: That's right. And there are plenty of people in the world who need our help. It's foolish not to use all our power to help them. We really don't have time to fight with one another.

COLETTE: You're right. You know, you've got some nice things in your house. Guess I haven't always appreciated them. But if you don't mind, I think I'll copy a few of your ideas for my place.

PATRICK: Go right ahead. I'm already making plans to use some of the things you've taught me.

COLETTE: Guess we all think we're too smart at times. We need to learn from each other. Oh, oh. Here come Ruth and Angus. *(They appear on stage.)* Now there's going to be an argument.

PATRICK: There always is. Let's stop here and listen. *(They move away from the front.)*

RUTH: Angus, I'm tired of arguing with you. Can't we be friends and just agree to disagree?

ANGUS: That would be a silly thing to do. If I'm friends with you, who'll I argue with?

RUTH: Don't you ever get tired of arguing and fighting?

ANGUS: No. I love to fight. I fight with everybody. *(Suddenly collapsing.)* Oh Ruth, I do get tired. But I've argued and fought for so long, I'm not sure I know how to be friends.

RUTH: Let's try, anyway.

ANGUS: All right. I'll give it a whirl. But don't expect too much.

RUTH: Don't worry, I won't. *(The others emerge and walk along.)* Why look, here are all the others. Peace and love to you.

NORMAN: Peace and love.

MARIA: A good greeting. Peace and love.

PATRICK: That goes for me too. Peace and love.

COLETTE: Don't forget me. Peace and love.

RUTH: How about it, Angus?

ANGUS: Oh, all right. Peace and love to everyone.

ALL THE OTHERS: Hurrah. Peace and love.

READER: Would you believe it? A new spirit is stirring at the crossroads of the world, or perhaps an old spirit is moving men's hearts again, the spirit of the great architect. Who knows what can happen when men say peace and love?

The Great Lover

Ephesians 5:25-27

Henry Ford once said, "History is bunk." By that he meant the events recorded aren't always the important ones and the records of historians are often false and biased. Perhaps he was right. But history is nevertheless important. You and I are the products of our history. We were born at a certain place and time, with special characteristics and interests because of what happened in the past history of our family. And we cannot change that past, though we can modify its effect upon us.

Churches also are the products of history. Denominations are what they are because of events that took place before any of the present leaders were born. Over 1900 years of history have passed since Christ "loved the church and gave his life for it" (TEV). During that period churches have divided and quarrels have been carried on for centuries.

104

Leaders have risen and died, leaving behind for good or ill the result of their leadership. And the history of the church may be bunk, but it has affected and still affects the church today.

There are always those who think that we can simply forget the past. Let's go back to the Bible, back to the time of Christ. Then we can all be brothers together again, they insist. But when we explore these invitations, we find that everyone has a different idea of what life was like in the early church and each idea is conditioned by history. So you can't escape it. The past tags along with us like an affectionate puppy.

Is there no hope? Are we doomed to be warring, quarreling Christians until the end of time? Do we just fool ourselves when we talk about friendship and even reunions among denominations? It is as foolish to predict the future as to try to escape the past. But there is one thing we can do. We can concentrate our gaze on Jesus Christ, the great Lover. And that's bound to have an effect on our relationship with other believers.

Note what our text tells us. *Christ loved the church.* He loved the church so much that he gave his life for it. And we must not simply put this love in the past tense. For Christ loves his church now. The church is his bride, his colony on this earth. And the term church certainly includes all true believers, all who acknowledge Jesus as Lord and Savior. There is no indication in the Bible that Jesus loves one section of his church, one denomination more than others. All are precious to him.

Sometimes in our pride we feel that our group is God's favorite. A certain proud churchman was told by the minister of another denomination that we both serve the same God. "Yes," replied the proud man, "you in your way and I in His." But that's nonsense. Neither sin and weakness nor love and faithfulness is limited to any denomination. Every Christian group has produced its saints and its villains. And the Lord who while he was here on earth showed great love for sinners has not turned his back on any group. We are a part of his church and he loves his church.

If only we can keep this picture of Jesus as the Great Lover in our mind, our relationship with fellow Christians will be easier. When the Corinthians began to split into warring groups, Paul reminded them that it was Christ who was crucified for them, not Paul or Peter or Apollos. And he told them that they were baptized in Jesus' name, not in the name of some earthly leader. The same truth applies today. God loves Methodists as much as Baptists, Roman Catholics as much as Lutherans, Pentecostals and Presbyterians alike. All have been baptized in Jesus' name and confess faith in the same Savior.

So, when we meet a fellow Christian of another denomination, our first reaction should be—this is someone whom Jesus loves. This is a man or woman for whom Christ died. If we begin by feeling—he's a Methodist and I'm a Lutheran, the walls of history immediately appear. But if we see the love of Christ embracing all, the denominational differences won't seem so significant.

The great preacher George Whitefield used to pause occasionally in a sermon and call dramatically: "How many Baptists are in heaven, how many Presbyterians, how many Lutherans?" Then he would give heaven's answer: "We don't know those names here." Of course that was an exaggeration but it does reflect the truth that Christ died for sinners, not for denominations. And he loves only one church, the fellowship of believers. We need to see this picture of the Great Lover, loving those for whom he died if we are to make any real progress in Christian fellowship and friendship.

But there is an almost frightening section in our text too. The author of Ephesians speaks of Christ wishing to sanctify his church so that she might be "without spot or wrinkle or any such thing, that she might be holy and without blemish." That's a fearful idea, for if there is anything the church has not been down through the ages, it is holy and without blemish. The history of denominational quarrels is ugly and evil. Often we have treated unbelievers with more love than we have those Christians who have dared disagree with us.

Without spot or blemish? Of course that is impossible in our present sinful world. Such a goal can only be achieved by the one who loves the church and gave his life for it. Nevertheless we can help by not hindering. We can let the spirit of Christ come in and fill our hearts with his love.

Suppose every Christian tried to show Christ's love toward all whom he met. Suppose that Lutherans and Presbyterians and Roman Catholics and all other groups tried to be guided by the simple question—What would Jesus have me do? The result would do more to bring denominations together than all the ecumenical meetings held by church leaders from now until the end of time. Of course that's an idealistic goal, but it is one that each of us can make his goal. Some of the pagans said of the early Christians: "See how these Christians love one another." How wonderful if people would say that again today.

We began by saying that we are the products of history. That's not a bad thing necessarily. We can all find reason to be proud of at least some of our history. The denominational badges we wear can reflect real zeal for the truth. But we dare not be the prisoners of history. Today the one who loves us calls us to show his love in word and deed to those around us.

Every good and perfect gift is from above, coming down from the Father of the heavenly lights, who does not change like shifting shadows.

The Best Blessing

CHARACTERS *Kevin Schrock*

FRANK BARNES: Fairly young business man, sensitive, somewhat confused. *Candy Bontrager*

JULIA BARNES: Housewife, more stable than husband FRANK. *Sam Maltzer*

DR. RAMON MOZANO: Young doctor from South America. *Donna Schrock*

MISS EDITH SARGENT: Young mission nurse from Africa. Not
a native.

SETTING

A typical living room with chairs for four people. Tables, etc.
can be added, depending on the space available.

(As the scene opens, FRANK BARNES *is reading the newspaper.* JULIA *comes into the room.)*

JULIA: Well, the turkey is getting brown and everything else seems to be cooking according to schedule. Think I'll sit down for a few minutes. *(She sits down.)* Are you getting hungry, Frank?

FRANK: *(Putting down his paper.)* Not really. As a matter of fact I was just about to come out to the kitchen and tell you I don't want any dinner today. A sandwich and a cup of coffee will be enough for me.

JULIA: *(Worried. Goes over to* FRANK.) Oh Frank, you're ill. And on Thanksgiving too! *(Feeling his forehead.)* Where do you hurt? It'll be hard to get a doctor today.

FRANK: *(Pushing her away.)* I don't need a doctor. I'm not sick. I simply don't want to eat a big dinner today. I'm not in the mood.

JULIA: *(Exasperated.)* Well, of all things. Here I've been working for the past two days getting everything ready for Thanksgiving and we're expecting company that we've never even seen before, and suddenly you're not in the *mood* for a big dinner. Frank I— *(Sits down, almost in tears.)*

FRANK: I know, I know. I'm being unreasonable. But it's mostly your fault.

JULIA: I could have guessed you'd say that. What have I done this time?

FRANK: Oh it's not really your fault. But you did insist that I go to church with you this morning and the sermon took away my appetite.

JULIA: Frank, that's a terrible thing to say about Rev. Wilson. I thought he had a good sermon today.

FRANK: Did you listen to what he said? Really listen?

JULIA: Of course I did. He said God has blessed us in this country and we ought to be very thankful for all we have received. And I think we should too.

FRANK: Strange, how we can both hear the same sermon and yet not hear the same sermon.

JULIA: What do *you* think he said?

FRANK: He said we Americans were better off than most people in the world. We have more food and more cars and better homes and bigger bank accounts than anybody else. So we ought to be grateful. But Julia, I refuse to be thankful because a lot of people are worse off than I am. And I don't think the Lord expects that kind of thankfulness.

JULIA: Frank, I don't think Rev. Wilson meant that.

FRANK: That's what I heard him say. He even mentioned that there are people here in America who don't have enough to eat, so we should consider ourselves fortunate if we can sit down to a good dinner today. And right there I lost my appetite.

JULIA: But I don't see what that has to do with our Thanksgiving dinner.

FRANK: Julia, I just can't sit down and eat turkey and dressing and mince pie and all the other goodies you're fixing. Every bite I would take today would remind me of the starving people in the rest of the world. They'll stand around our table like hungry animals, their big eyes looking at me while I shovel in the food, I just can't do it.

JULIA: Frank, I know how you feel. But none of those people will have one more bite to put in their stomachs whether you eat dinner today or not. You can't fly our turkey to Africa or Asia.

FRANK: I know that. When I was little and didn't want to eat my vegetables, mother would always say there were thousands of Chinese boys and girls that would love to have what I left on my plate. I couldn't understand why it was always Chinese who wanted my vegetables. I always said, tell them to come and get them but no one ever appeared. Julia, I know I'm being foolish, but I can't help it.

JULIA: Well, I'm not going to make you eat. But we do have guests coming so you'll have to make some excuse for your peculiar taste. Or absence of taste, I suppose I should say. *(Knock on the door.)* There they are now. You go to the door. I'll take my apron off and be right back. *(Starts to exit.)*

FRANK: All right, dear. And I'll try not to embarrass you. *(Opens the door.)*

DR. MOZANO: Is this the residence of Mr. and Mrs. Barnes? *(No effort should be made for* MOZANO *to talk with an accent.)*

FRANK: You've come to the right place. You're the students from the medical college, aren't you?

MISS SARGENT: That's right.

FRANK: Fine. Come right in. We're expecting you. *(They enter.)*

DR. MOZANO: Thank you. Permit me to introduce myself. I am Dr. Ramon Mozano and this is Miss Edith Sargent.

FRANK: Happy to have you. I'm Frank Barnes *(Shakes hands as* JULIA *enters.)* and this is my wife Julia. Julia, this is Edith Sargent and Dr. Ramon Moz—

DR. MOZANO: Mozano. It's a strange name to you Americans.

JULIA: *(Shaking hands.)* I'm pleased to meet both of you. Won't you please sit down. Dinner will be ready in a little while.

(All four sit down, the two men in the middle, the women out of the center.)

DR. MOZANO: Thank you. It was so nice of you to invite two students from the medical college to have Thanksgiving dinner with you.

MISS SARGENT: It certainly was. School can be a bit lonely over a holiday.

JULIA: We're just happy to have you. We don't have any family of our own and when the church bulletin asked for people who would like to have foreign students in their homes today, we signed up right away.

MISS SARGENT: Well, we're the hungry foreigners who were assigned to you.

FRANK: *(Has been thinking.)* Mozano. Are you from South America, Doctor?

DR. MOZANO: Yes sir. I'm a doctor from a small village in the Andes Mountains. The government gave me a year's leave to study here in America so that I can get some special training.

FRANK: I see. And you, Miss Sargent. Your name doesn't sound foreign. Are you an American?

MISS SARGENT: My parents are American, Mr. Barnes, or were, at least. They've been missionaries in Africa for many years and I suppose by now they'd call Africa home. I was born and educated there, so this is my first trip to America. I'm taking some special nurses' training at the medical school so I can go back and help in the hospital at the mission station.

JULIA: I suppose Thanksgiving isn't a completely strange holiday for you then.

MISS SARGENT: Not entirely, although we didn't have any turkey and dressing and the other things that go with an American thanksgiving.

FRANK: I guess it has become pretty much of a feast day for us. Feast and football.

DR. MOZANO: I can't blame you for the feasting. You certainly have lots of food and other good things in this country.

JULIA: Is that how America impresses you, Dr. Mozano?

DR. MOZANO: Yes. I had read about your wealth before I came. But like the Queen of Sheba, the half hadn't been told me. Your cities are overwhelming. The cars, the buildings, the money.

JULIA: Don't you have some wealthy people in your homeland too?

DR. MOZANO: Oh yes. There are wealthy people in every land. But we do not have so many as here.

FRANK: We have some poor people too, even some who won't be having a fancy dinner this Thanksgiving.

DR. MOZANO: I'm sure you do. But to my eyes, even the poor people here seem rich.

JULIA: How strange. Miss Sargent, do you get the same impression of us?

FRANK: Yes. Do we look like overstuffed pigs to you too?

DR. MOZANO: Oh, I did not say that.

FRANK: I know you didn't. I did.

MISS SARGENT: I am impressed by what I see here. My parents tried to tell me what America would be like but I'm afraid they've been away from here too long. At least I wasn't prepared for what I've seen. The stores, especially the shopping centers fascinate me. They seem like fairyland, or perhaps I should say Vanity Fair.

FRANK: Won't you both find it hard to go back home and leave all this behind?

DR. MOZANO: I keep telling myself—no. My people need me. But I'll admit it may be a bit difficult when the time comes.

MISS SARGENT: I haven't wrestled with the problem yet. But life is always coming and going, leaving pleasant things and finding other pleasant things. I think I'll be ready to return to Africa when the time comes.

FRANK: You know, I think it's providential that you two were assigned to us. Before you came, I was having a little personal problem about Thanksgiving and you two may be able to help me.

JULIA: (Alarmed.) Frank, don't bother our guests with your queer ideas.

FRANK: But I must. Maybe they are the very ones who can give me the answer.

DR. MOZANO: I'm sure we will be glad to help if you'll tell us the problem. But if it's medical, we aren't licensed to practice here.

FRANK: Oh, nothing like that. But let me ask you some questions first, Dr. Mozano. You've seen our wealth here in America. Doesn't it make you angry at times?

DR. MOZANO: Angry? How do you mean?

FRANK: Well, we're only one nation among a lot of others. Why should we have so much to be thankful for and other people have so little?

DR. MOZANO: That's a strange question for an American to ask.

FRANK: I suppose it is. But today I'm asking it. I'm wondering how I can sit down to a big Thanksgiving dinner when half the world is starving.

DR. MOZANO: That is a hard question, Mr. Barnes. But you must not ask me to speak. I am a guest in your house.

JULIA: Frank, stop this. You're embarrassing Dr. Mozano.

FRANK: But I want an honest answer. Doesn't it seem wrong, Dr. Mozano, that God blesses us so much and gives your people so little?

DR. MOZANO: I—I—

FRANK: *(Relentlessly.)* Tell me. Does everyone in your little Andean village have enough to eat every day?

DR. MOZANO: *(Agitated. Getting up and pacing the floor.)* No, no, they don't. Mr. and Mrs. Barnes, I have seen children in my clinic, their stomachs distended by starvation, their bodies permanently stunted by lack of adequate food.

FRANK: Well, we have people in clinics here too, people who are too fat because they get too much to eat. We have people who don't just feast on Thanksgiving but every day. Doesn't that upset you?

DR. MOZANO: Yes, yes of course it does.

FRANK: Well, tell me. What's wrong with such a world? Do we have a right to be thankful because we're better off than others, better fed, better housed, richer, fatter?

DR. MOZANO: You goad me, Mr. Barnes. All right, I'll say it. I don't understand why the world's like this. I look at your well-fed people and I wish I had never come here, even though everyone is nice to me. I sit down and eat and then I think of what the people in my village are having for dinner and I almost choke on my food. You asked me whether it will be hard to go back. Yes, it will, not because I want to stay here but because my people have so little and I can't take back with me even a small part of your abundance.

FRANK: Ha. There *is* someone who agrees with me. I told my wife I couldn't eat dinner today because I couldn't feel thankful just because I had more than other people.

DR. MOZANO: I'm afraid I can't eat your dinner either after this conversation. I would see the little children and the old people, pleading for a morsel of food. (*Sinks into chair and buries his head in his hands.*)

JULIA: Oh dear, there go all my Thanksgiving preparations.

MISS SARGENT: May I say something?

FRANK: Of course. Dr. Mozano and I were so wrapped up in our discussion that I'm afraid we forgot you, Miss Sargent. I'm sorry. But you must feel the same way we do. Your people in Africa don't have too much to eat either, do they?

MISS SARGENT: No. There's famine there too. And I don't think anyone should be thankful just because they have more than others do.

FRANK: Sounds like the Pharisee in the parable, doesn't it. I thank thee that I am not as other men are, hungry and ill-fed . . .

MISS SARGENT: Exactly. But let me tell you something that happened when I was a little girl. We didn't have a hospital on the mission station then, so my father had to dispense some simple remedies to the people and try to help them as best he could when they got sick.

FRANK: He couldn't do that here.

MISS SARGENT: I suppose not. But there was no one

else to help. One day I was fed up with all the sick natives coming to the house and interrupting our dinner and even our sleep. So I said to my father—send them away. But my father said, no, let's be thankful for sick people.

FRANK: Thankful that people were sick?

MISS SARGENT: That's what I thought he meant. Then he explained. Sickness was there before we came. It would probably be there when we were gone. But we must be thankful for the opportunity to help others while we can.

JULIA: That's a different approach.

MISS SARGENT: I think it's the right one. My father insisted that a person should be most thankful when there were others to be helped and you have the power to help them.

DR. MOZANO: But he wasn't a trained doctor.

MISS SARGENT: I know. And it grieved him when they brought someone who was beyond his skill to heal. That's why he worked day and night to get a hospital built close to our mission station. And that's why I'm here in America now, to learn more about nursing. I think this Thanksgiving means a lot to me today because soon I'm going to go back to Africa and help the people in that hospital. And that will please my father more than anything I've ever done.

DR. MOZANO: Your father must be a remarkable man and I think he has a remarkable daughter.

MISS SARGENT: He is a remarkable man. He says it is always better to light a candle than to curse the darkness.

FRANK: *(Beginning to see the light.)* You're not telling us all this so we can appreciate your father's work. It's meant to say something about my problem, isn't it?

MISS SARGENT: I think it does. It seems to me, Mr. Barnes, that you *do* have a real reason to be thankful in America today, not because you have more food or automobiles or money than other people but because you have more opportunities to help others in the world. You can feed the hungry and heal the sick and bring hope to the helpless. And that's the best blessing of all.

FRANK: *(Musing.)* Opportunity to help others. The best blessing. Miss Sargent, you're right. And I've just been cursing the darkness. Dr. Mozano, there's no reason why you have to go home empty-handed. Your people need help. Well, I can help. Our church can help. We can send you food and agricultural experts to train your people to raise better crops. Things don't have to remain the same as they were when you left.

DR. MOZANO: Do you mean it?

FRANK: Of course I mean it. Why, this Thanksgiving

can mean a real opportunity for all of us. The start of many wonderful opportunities. Miss Sargent, you're the best preacher I ever heard.

MISS SARGENT: No, Mr. Barnes. I'm simply a person who has learned that real thankfulness comes from using opportunities to help others.

JULIA: Look, I hate to interrupt all the fine talk but I think my dinner will be ready in a few minutes. Is anybody going to eat it?

FRANK: Of course we are.

DR. MOZANO: I will eat with great joy today.

JULIA: Good. Then give me a few minutes and then everyone into the dining room. And bring your appetites. *(Exit. The others sit for a minute and then exit.)*

The Source of It All

James 1:17

One of the favorite routines used by comedians is the "That's good, that's bad" joke. You know how it goes. The comedian relates something that has happened to him. "That's good," says the stooge. "No, that's bad," is the reply. Then when an explanation has been made, the stooge says, "That's bad," whereupon the joke is reversed and the comedian insists: "No, that's good," and so on. This is usually a boring routine since we all know the pattern, but behind the joke is a rather challenging truth. Life is so full of uncertainties that we have trouble deciding what is good and what is bad for us.

Thus one man makes a fortune in business and it proves to be a blessing to him and his whole family. Another man is equally successful but the added money and prestige changes his affection for his wife and alienates and spoils his children. One man's busi-

ness fails and he ends up a suicide; another has the
same experience but emerges from the failure a
stronger and better man.

The world has a simple answer for the "that's good,
that's bad" routine. The world says it's luck. One man
is lucky, the other is unlucky. One man has the
golden touch, the other would be caught with only
a fork if it were raining soup. Belief in luck is probably the most widespread belief among human
beings. Lady Luck is the goddess for millions and
they all wonder how to win her favor.

The Christian does not believe in luck. He insists
that the world is ruled by God, not by blind chance.
Yet all of us have difficulties with the vagaries of
life. One day we have that "good day" that everybody wishes for us; the next day everything goes
wrong. One Thanksgiving we can think of a dozen
things to praise God for; the next year we are hard
put to remember one. What's the matter? If God
rules this world, is he a fickle God, dispensing his
favors at random?

No one can give a complete explanation of why
things happen to us in this life. The most fruitless
task in the world is of trying to justify God's ways
to man. As Paul reminds us, we in this life see
through a glass darkly. Nevertheless, there are some
things we can say about God and the blessings which
he gives us. And the first thing is that God is *not* a
fickle God. He loves us with a steadfast love. Regard-
less of what events may seem to say, God does not
love us one day and hate us the next. James says he

is "The Father of lights with whom there is no varia-
tion or shadow due to change." This same truth is
reflected in Psalm 136 with its monotonous but re-
assuring refrain: "His steadfast love endures forever."

This doesn't mean that the Christian does not have
to face some unpleasant things in life. We all have
good days and bad days. Even Jesus experienced
times of great success and also periods when many
of his followers deserted him. In this life we do have
to face up to many unpleasant things. Paul partially
explains this when he insists that all things *work
together* for good to those who love the Lord. He
does not say all things are good. But the misfortunes
of life should never obscure for us the goodness of
God. He loves us and seeks only to bless us.

A second truth is this: there are times when we
are especially blessed and may feel particularly
thankful to God. All of us have experienced such occasions. A loved one recovers from a dangerous ill-
ness. A young person graduates from college and is
ready for his or her chosen profession. A married
couple celebrate many years of happiness together.
At such times we know what James is talking about
when he speaks of "every good endowment and every
perfect gift is from above."

The Christian certainly has cause to feel thankful when such events occur and it is proper for us
to express our thanks in worship and praise. Long
before the American holiday, Thanksgiving Day was
inaugurated, people of God gave thanks for special
blessings. The children of Israel had their times of

special thanksgiving as did Christians down through the centuries. Such customs are good, provided they don't make us forget the unceasing, daily goodness of God. In the words of the 23rd psalm: "Surely goodness and mercy shall follow me *all* the days of my life."

But we still have the problem of the "that's good, that's bad" routine. How do we explain the fact that the same type of event may help one man and harm another? Perhaps part of the difficulty lies in too narrow a definition of God's gifts. James gives us no specific description of what a gift from God may be. The truth of the matter is that almost every event that occurs in our life has this good-bad possibility. The happenings of each day can draw us closer to God or drive us away from him.

An old hymn proclaims: "Count your blessings, name them one by one." The advice is good provided we do not limit our idea of what may be called a blessing. Few would include troubles or difficulties under this heading and yet at times such events can be real helps. No one should be expected to be thankful for sickness or business failure yet when we look back on our lives, let's be honest enough to admit that some of these things may be included in the good things that come from God.

And while we are talking about a broader definition of blessing, let us also see that we need to be thankful for opportunities to help others. We aren't inclined to take such a view of course. Many agree with the quip: "A friend in need is a friend to avoid."

Yet often our greatest joy comes when we use the good gifts from God to assist others. To be able to help is a privilege. The giver must learn to say thank you to God, just as much as the receiver does.

Thanksgiving day then is a proper day in the Christian calendar. It is right that we should worship in our churches on this day. It is good that families meet together and recall the blessings of the past year. But thanksgiving is really a lifelong matter. The whole life of a Christian should be seen as a giving of thanks to the One who gives us every good and perfect gift.

MORE RESOURCES FOR DRAMA
AND PREACHING BY W. A. POOVEY

Let Us Adore Him: Dramas and Meditations for Advent, Christmas, Epiphany

Signs of His Coming: Dramas and Meditations for Advent, Christmas, Epiphany

Six Faces of Lent: Judas, Caiaphas, Pilate, Barabbas, Peter, Dismas

What Did Jesus Do? Meditations and Dramas for Lent

Cross Words: Lenten Sermons and Dramas for Church Presentation

Mustard Seeds and Wineskins: Dramas and Meditations on Seven Parables

Banquets and Beggars: Dramas and Meditations on Six Parables

Stand Still and Move Ahead: Meditations on Ephesians

The Power of the Kingdom: Meditations on Matthew